Well Equipped

Well Equipped

A Practical Survival Guide for Pastors and Volunteers Who Work with Children and Teens in Church Settings

Jennifer Coles Hill

RESOURCE *Publications* • Eugene, Oregon

WELL EQUIPPED
A Practical Survival Guide for Pastors and Volunteers Who Work with Children and Teens in Church Settings

Copyright © 2024 Jennifer Coles Hill. All rights reserved. Except for brief quotations in critical publications or reviews, no part of this book may be reproduced in any manner without prior written permission from the publisher. Write: Permissions, Wipf and Stock Publishers, 199 W. 8th Ave., Suite 3, Eugene, OR 97401.

Resource Publications
An Imprint of Wipf and Stock Publishers
199 W. 8th Ave., Suite 3
Eugene, OR 97401

www.wipfandstock.com

PAPERBACK ISBN: 979-8-3852-2865-2
HARDCOVER ISBN: 979-8-3852-2866-9
EBOOK ISBN: 979-8-3852-2867-6

VERSION NUMBER 09/05/24

The information provided in this book is designed to provide helpful guidance on the subject matter. However, it is not meant to diagnose or treat any medical or psychological condition and should not serve as a substitute for professional advice from a physician, therapist, or other treatment professional. The practices described in this book should be applied by the reader in consultation with qualified professionals as well as the student's parents. Although the author and publisher have made every effort to ensure accuracy, information and suggestions included in the book may change as new research becomes available.

All Scripture quotations, unless otherwise indicated, are taken from the Holy Bible, New International Version®, NIV®. Copyright ©1973, 1978, 1984, 2011 by Biblica, Inc.™ Used by permission of Zondervan. All rights reserved worldwide. www.zondervan.com The "NIV" and "New International Version" are trademarks registered in the United States Patent and Trademark Office by Biblica, Inc.™

For Tanner and Alisa

May the Lord continue to bless your ministries, not because of who you are, but because of who He is in you.

Contents

Acknowledgments | ix
Introduction | xi

1. Learning and Development | 1
2. Planning Lessons | 13
3. Managing Behaviors | 31
4. IEPs and 504 Plans | 44
5. Autism and ADHD | 51
6. Language and Culture | 67
7. Poverty and Trauma | 83
8. Depression and Anxiety | 104
9. Reflective Listening and Boundaries | 119

Bibliography | 129

Acknowledgments

THE IDEA FOR THIS book was born after a presentation that I made at Northwest Nazarene University's Wesley Center Conference about working with special needs students in the church. The feedback and requests to share session information that I received afterward helped me catch a glimpse of how limited resources are in this area specifically for pastors and volunteers in church settings. I am grateful for the encouragement of Pastor Heather Pillers and Pastor Drew Vinson, who were the first people that I shared the idea with over lunch in the university cafeteria.

The pages and chapters that lie ahead could only have been researched and written down thanks to the sabbatical semester that I was granted by NNU. For months, my home office was filled with the faces and stories of thousands of students I have had the privilege of working with over the last three decades. Their struggles and triumphs gave me purpose for this work.

Thank you to Matthew Wimer and the crew at Wipf and Stock Publishers who made this book possible after several other publishing houses were not sure how it would fit in their markets. Thanks also to Dana Patterson and Ella Noland who served as my gracious and talented copyeditors—always on the lookout for silly spellings and two spaces after a period!

Special thanks to my family, whose constant love and encouragement continues to be my inspiration. My parents, Bill and Karen Coles, have been my cheerleaders from the very beginning, always

ACKNOWLEDGMENTS

being supportive by simply showing up and being available. My husband, Cary, helps bring organization to all my crazy ideas and continues to be a steady source of strength through every mountain and valley we face. Our incredible adult children, Tanner and Alisa, were some of my first readers and helpful springboards for ideas and more accurate next-gen terminology. I am also grateful to our small group, church family, and the NNU College of Education that prayed me through this entire process from the early days of brainstorming to final publication. I feel incredibly fortunate to be able to have all of you in my corner!

Introduction

> "... so that the servant of God may be well equipped
> for every good work." 2 Timothy 3:17 NIV

IF THIS BOOK HAS found its way to you, it is likely you are either currently working with children or teens in a church or Christian non-profit setting, or you are contemplating the possibility of getting involved. Thank you! Your unique talents and gifts are desperately needed, and there is a place ready and waiting for you to serve right now.

The summer after my freshman year in college, I was a counselor for 10 straight weeks of church camp. During the orientation, our director emphasized that working with kids and teens was not difficult—all we needed to do was "share what we know." While the sentiment of that statement was encouraging, in my head I was screaming, "But I do not know anything yet!" I had completed two introductory education and psychology classes which simply served to remind me that my journey had just begun, and I still had a lot to learn. Thankfully, no campers were seriously harmed that summer, and I am sure that God used my inadequacies more than I realized. However, I will never forget how it felt to be completely willing to be used by God but have absolutely *no idea* what I was doing.

Fast forward about 30 years ... Now it is my own two children who are spending their college summers working at church camps and preparing for careers in different areas of ministry. The idea for this book was to write down for them (and others) all that I have learned about working with kids and teens in my career as a teacher and counselor. Nothing here is rocket science and very little is original, but it is a collection of tools, information, and practical advice to help you be better equipped to serve, whether you are working in a paid pastoral position or volunteering your time.

A note about theology: This book is not intended to show you *what* to teach, but rather, *how* to teach it. It is best to begin by understanding the doctrine of your specific church or parachurch organization as the initial framework. Then, use the ideas in this book to make that theology come alive by connecting it with your students in ways that they understand and will remember. The beautiful thing is the Holy Spirit serves as our instructional coach, so we are never truly on our own in our work with kids.

My prayer is that the ideas in this book will help equip you for the most important work you will ever do—helping young people meet, know, and share Jesus in real and life-changing ways.

1

Learning and Development

"Day after day, in the temple courts and from house to house, they never stopped teaching and proclaiming the good news that Jesus is the Messiah." Acts 5:42 NIV

LET'S BEGIN BY THINKING about thinking. The human mind is fascinating, and neuroscience gives us a glimpse of the beautiful and complex ways that God has created how we each discern and comprehend the world around us. Science shows us how we are wired to process information, but how do we then take that information and make meaning with it? In the early 20th century, cognitive psychologists like Dewey, Vygotsky, and Piaget helped contribute to the age-old conversation—How do we learn? Their findings, and most of our modern-day teacher training, are built around the idea that each learner has to construct their own understanding of an idea in order for it to be retained. This means that our prior knowledge and cognitive structure, the patterns our brain uses to organize and maintain information and perceptions, contribute directly to how well we can absorb and grasp a concept. This is why different people can be presented with the same information and walk away with very different understandings.

It becomes the role of the teacher, leader, facilitator, or pastor to create experiences that help participants connect the new information to what they already know. The more that the learner can do the learning, as opposed to passively sitting and listening, the more they will understand and retain. This type of teaching takes time and planning, because it takes longer to explore a topic than just hear about it, so it is important to decide which ideas or concepts are the most important and focus on bringing big ideas to life.

I recently taught a Sunday school lesson to first graders focused on Matthew 13, Jesus's teachings about the kingdom of God. That is a difficult passage for adults to comprehend, let alone six-year olds! I sat down with the lesson a few days before I was supposed to teach it and tried to decide what was the most important thing that I wanted the kids to remember. What did they already know that I could connect it to? How could I build upon that knowledge in a way that they would remember?

I decided to get out my son's old wooden castle that we played with for hours when he was little. It took a little maneuvering to get it down the stairs into the first grade classroom at church, but when the students entered, they were automatically intrigued. "What a cool castle!" and, "Do we get to play with that today?" were some of the comments that I heard as they came into the room. As they sat down in a circle around the castle, I asked them what they already knew about kingdoms.

"Who is in charge of a kingdom?" I asked.

"A king," they quickly replied.

I took out one of my son's king action figures and put it on one of the spires. "What else might we find in a kingdom?" They responded with a list of things like horses, princesses, a moat, and, my favorite, a fire-breathing dragon!

Then, I shared with them that Jesus once told his disciples and a crowd of people what the kingdom of God was like. For each illustration from the parable, our children's pastor had graciously prepared some items for me to use—a jar of mustard seeds, a packet of yeast, a pearl necklace, and a jar of gold coins (which, to their dismay, were just plastic). Most of these items had little personal connection for them, so I had to build some background.

"A mustard seed is very small," I said as I put one in each of their hands. "Can something this small do very much?" Most of them replied, "No."

"But what happens when you plant a seed into the ground?"

"It grows!" many of them answered quickly.

"Exactly," I said. "So, Jesus wanted the people to know that the kingdom of God would start out small, but then grow and spread all across the world."

"So even outside the castle?" one student responded.

"Yes!" I exclaimed, excited that they were catching on and making connections.

I took the jar of mustard seed and put it on the castle turret where they could all see it. Then we talked about yeast, the ingredient that transforms dough and helps it rise.

"This is a packet of yeast, each granule is small too, like a mustard seed. But when you put yeast into something, a change happens."

At this point I decided not to open the packet, since they already had a mustard seed in their hands, and it could get too messy if I poured it out, so instead I walked around and shook the packet so that they could hear what was inside.

"Have you ever seen dough rise?" At this point only a few acted like they knew what I was talking about, so I gave a few examples of rolls, bread, and pizza dough rising before it is baked.

"We can't see the yeast inside after it is stirred in, but we know it is working because the dough gets bigger. So, if Jesus said that the kingdom of God changes things, and if it is in us and in our world, what does that mean?"

"I'm going to puff up like a donut!" one of my favorite kids shouted.

"Maybe," I said with a smile. "But even if you don't get puffier, the idea is that you will be changed, like a transformer." (Thankfully, they mostly understood this pop culture reference!)

I put the packet of yeast on another turret and we did the same things with the pearl necklace and jar of coins.

"To God, you are a priceless part of the kingdom and God keeps searching for you until he finds you. In the same way, God wants you to search for him like you would search for a great treasure. The kingdom of God is something that you can experience now, and is the greatest quest that is worth devoting your life to."

"Like a quest for the knights?" my donut kid asked.

"You've got it," I smiled.

By the time we were finished, we had the mustard seed container, yeast packet, pearl necklace, and jar of coins all sitting on the castle turrets. Now it was time to review, which is a crucial piece of understanding.

"Why did Jesus say that his kingdom was like mustard seed?"

"What does yeast tell us about his kingdom?"

"Why is God, our King, willing to search for you like a priceless pearl?"

"Why does God want us to search for him and his kingdom like a buried treasure or knight's quest?"

As the lesson concluded, I was relieved that this approach had worked! "Now when you think about God's kingdom, how are you going to think about it differently than you do about other kinds of kingdoms?" Their thoughtful answers that followed helped me know that they understood the big ideas.

After a coloring page and fun activity, I had them each say one thing that Jesus used to describe his kingdom as they gave me a high five and exited the room. Mustard seed was the favorite answer, and I knew that several of them were still gripping that tiny little seed in their other hand as they left the classroom.

As you look back over this example, consider how I accomplished the following objectives:

1. Determine the most important idea of the story that I really wanted my students to remember.

2. Think about what prior knowledge they may already have and find ways to build upon that knowledge.

3. Plan ways to make learning engaging and hands on using manipulatives, pictures, games, etc.
4. Find several different ways to check for understanding and make sure that they "got it" by the end of the lesson.

Obviously, this lesson was created for first graders, so the goal was to take complex ideas and break them down into manageable chunks. However, the process does not change that much as you work with older kids.

As we are thinking about learning, it is important to remember that developmental levels play a role in what kids are able to understand and remember. There will always be outliers at the extreme ends, but take a little time and consider what the developmental levels are of the kids you are currently working with or may be working with in the future.

Erikson's Eight Stages of Development

There are a lot of different theories and levels of childhood development out there. In my counseling program, I was introduced to Erik Erikson and his eight developmental phases[1] that are based on conflicts and challenges at different points of life. This idea really resonated with me and helped me better understand the students that I was working with in a school counseling setting. How successfully we develop qualities to navigate these essential conflicts at different times in our lives makes a major difference in how we each see the world.

Trust vs. Mistrust (Birth to 18 months)

The most important learning for an infant is if he or she can trust the world. This is typically learned through a loving and protective relationship with parents and caregivers. This is also not an all-or-nothing process. A baby is not completely trusting or completely

---

1. Erikson, *Identity and the Life Cycle.*

mistrusting in every situation. A healthy amount of mistrust can prepare us to be cautious and self-protective when needed later on. However, it is vitally important at this stage that healthy and trusting relationships outweigh untrustworthy relationships. The big question at this stage for infants is the following: "Is the world safe or something to be afraid of?"

Autonomy vs. Shame and Doubt (18 months to three years)

As babies grow, they develop a need for independence and control. This is normal and important! They are able to do more things for themselves and need to begin to develop a basic confidence in their own abilities (i.e. feeding themselves and potty training). By the way, this is also why so many toddlers love to shout the word "no" as they begin to want to do things their own way. Some level of independence is important at this stage so toddlers develop autonomy at appropriate levels. For example, giving toddlers choices like what they want to wear, read, or have for a snack is empowering. (Even if it means some mismatched clothes!) While there is always a place for healthy discipline, parents and caregivers need to be very cautious about being overly controlling or chastising their toddler to the point that the child feels ashamed about themselves or their conduct. The developmental question is, "Can I do things for myself, or am I reliant on others?"

Initiative vs. Guilt (Preschool, ages three to five)

At this stage, children gain an understanding of the world through exploration and play. Being encouraged to try new activities and experiences is important, as well as being applauded for imagination and creativity. Kids who do not develop a sense of their own initiative and purpose may become fearful of trying new things. Parents and caregivers should allow children the ability to make appropriate choices and face reasonable challenges while still maintaining safe boundaries. When initiative efforts are stifled, kids may experience embarrassment and feel that they are somehow a bad person. Caring adults can help combat this by helping children see mistakes as learning opportunities, and continue to encourage practice and persistence. The key question for this stage is, "Am I good or bad?"

Industry vs. Inferiority (Middle years, ages six to 11)

This fourth stage is one that children begin to wrestle with as they enter formalized schooling. Social influences increase dramatically, whereas previously, interactions centered mainly on family and caregivers. Friends and classmates begin to play a major role, and likely, for the first time, talents and abilities are measured against those of others. Think of the term industry here as industriousness or confidence. Students who do well in school, at church, or in other activities develop a sense of competence and a greater sense of self-esteem. Those who receive little or no encouragement or support begin to doubt their abilities and may begin feeling a sense of failure and incompetence. The key question at this stage is, "How can I be good?"

Identity vs. Confusion (Teen years from 12-18)

This stage will be of no surprise to parents, youth pastors, and church volunteers who work with teens. During this time, adolescents are developing a sense of self and independence as they wrestle with social relationships. The major question at this stage is, "Who am I?" Lacking a sense of identity, known as role confusion, can lead to difficulties with commitment, poor mental health, a weak sense of self, and a lack of confidence.[2] However, it is much easier to talk about the results of role confusion as opposed to the factors that help teens develop a strong self-identity, because the factors can be so multi-faceted. Identity involves relationships, beliefs, values, memories, and experiences

2. Rageliene, "Links of Adolescents Identity Development," 97-105.

that contribute to a sense of self. The good news here is that as our churches help our teens discover who they are in Christ and the plans that he has for their lives, we can help strengthen their identities and point them to who they are meant to be.

Intimacy vs. Isolation (Young adults from 18-40)

The basic virtue of Erikson's sixth stage is love. The guiding question for this time of life is, "Will I be loved, or will I be alone?" It is vital for our development that we have close, committed relationships with other people, and we are more likely to do this if we have developed a strong sense of self. While this idea of intimacy is typically framed by our society in the context of marriage, it does not have to be exclusive to a marriage relationship. Erikson described closeness, honesty, and love as characteristics of intimate relationships. Adults who can navigate this stage successfully are able to create fulfilling relationships with other people and truly care for others. Sadly, the consequences of extended isolation can lead to serious negative emotional and physical health.

Generativity vs. Stagnation (Middle age from 40-65)

While this book is not designed to focus on the stages past adolescence, it is worth noting the last two of Erikson's conflicts because they may apply directly to where you are, or where the volunteers in your church may be. Important events at this stage are parenthood and work. The major guiding question for this stage is, "How can I contribute to the world?" which may be a reason some volunteers in your church have enlisted to help out. At this time, middle-aged adults strive to nurture things that will outlast themselves, which is why positive contributions to society or church settings can be so rewarding. Erikson believed that participating in the lives of others brings greater fulfillment and ultimately leads to feelings of productivity and inclusion. If this was not reason enough to bolster your volunteer list, we must also consider the flip side and the consequences of stagnation—reduced cognitive function, poorer health, and decreased life satisfaction. Which camp do you want to find yourself in?

Integrity vs. Despair (Older adulthood from 65 on)

The final stage of Erikson's theory begins approximately at retirement and ends ultimately at death. The basic virtue here is wisdom, and the major question is, "Did I lead a meaningful life?" Integrity, in this sense, is about accomplishment and fulfillment—a feeling of peace and a sense of success. Unfortunately, we have all known senior citizens who fall on the despair continuum, vacillating between regret, bitterness, complaining, and general grouchiness. However, our churches miss a valuable opportunity when we do not connect the older and younger members of our congregations together, something that can be mutually beneficial to each group.

Middle School

I had always pictured myself as a high school teacher, but when I received a job offer to teach seventh-grade language arts a few months before my college graduation, I was thrilled to have a job lined up, no matter the level! What I quickly discovered was just how much fun middle school students can be. While many youth groups may be a combination of both middle school and high school levels, there are some important distinctions to remember developmentally when working with the two different age groups.

Adolescence (usually from age 10-19) can be a tumultuous time for our students. They are moving from concrete to abstract thinking and their brains are growing at tremendous rates. This development is crucial to begin the ability to plan, problem solve, think critically, and control impulses. This rapid brain development can also affect short-term memory. A middle schooler can typically only retain five or six bits of information at a time, so it is important to break things down into more manageable chunks (content, directions, etc.) and provide limited amounts of new information at a time. Lesson variety with a high level of student involvement and hands-on learning actually helps stimulate brain pathways!

As with all developmental changes, students begin a grade level at different points and some cycle through stages more quickly than others. Some may be ready for higher problem solving, and others may need more concrete information. As Peter Lorain, a retired high school teacher and middle school principal emphasizes, "The middle school classroom should be an active, stimulating place where people talk and share, movement is common and planned for, and the teacher uses a wide array of approaches to introduce, model, and reinforce learning."[3]

The good news is that middle school students tend to be willing to take risks and have a curiosity and eagerness to explore new ideas. They have less inhibitions to be silly and are usually eager to ask questions. They can also have intense interests in topics for short periods of time, so be warned, a really "cool" topic or fad can burn out quickly, even from one week to the next. The energy and enthusiasm from your middle schoolers will both exhilarate and exhaust you at times! Remember too that this group of students can get distracted easily and their ability to practice self-discipline is not fully formed yet, so helping them stay organized and use time well will reap great rewards as they continue to mature.

The year that my daughter turned 13, she was making some choices that seemed out of character. I was in the middle of cancer treatment and I knew that she was carrying a lot of friendship struggles on her own and trying to protect me from the details so I would not worry. I will never forget the conversation in which I remarked, "Honey, I am just trying to figure you out right now." She turned to me with tears in her eyes and said, brutally honestly, "Mom, I am trying to figure myself out right now too!" I needed her to remind me in that moment (and for the next seven years) that growing up and navigating adolescence was not easy, and she was trying her best to figure herself and the world out as well.

---

3. Lorain, "Brain Development in Young Adolescents," 1-2.

High School

High school students as a group tend to be more independent and can have a more serious or focused approach to subjects that they are interested in. Critical thinking and problem solving become easier for them as they approach adulthood. Encouraging your high schoolers to engage in deeper critical thinking and problem solving will not only increase their learning, but also will increase their confidence in their own abilities.

High schoolers may also be taking on more responsibilities at home, school, and work which may limit the time that they can commit to church activities. Finding ways for your youth staff to stay connected with students during a very busy time in their lives can help them stay connected to your youth group or church family even when they are not able to attend on a regular basis. I know of several churches that maintain a calendar of activities that their students are involved in. Having your youth pastor show up to a band concert or having an entire church cheering section at a basketball game is incredibly encouraging to a student. For those who work a lot of hours outside of school, see if you can bring them coffee on a lunch break or find out if your local high school has an open campus where you can check in as a visitor and bring a group of students pizza for lunch.

As students get closer to graduation, they also start to carry an enormous burden to figure out what they want to do with the rest of their lives. Do everything you can to focus on the present. As my daughter was getting ready to start her senior year in high school, I remember a conversation after church where she said to me—"Why does everyone keep asking me where I am going to go to college and what I am going to major in? I wish that they would just ask me what I am looking forward to in my senior year!" While I tried to remind her that people in our church were just being friendly and making conversation with her, it also convicted me a little as I started to realize just how often that was the first question I asked seniors as well.

The Strength is in the Relationship

Now that we have discussed some of the basics of learning and child development, it is important to talk about the power of relationships, because it guides everything else that we will discuss. Early on in my teacher training, I had a professor that often reminded us: "They do not care how much you know, until they know how much you care." While that specific saying is not used as much today, the sentiment is timeless.

Kids who have a loving, caring adult in their lives, whether that be a parent, grandparent, youth volunteer, children's pastor, or [insert your role here], are far more likely to navigate the difficult storms of childhood and adolescents successfully. Healthy relationships between students and their peers, teachers, family, and church can make all of the difference between a child who develops a positive self-concept and believes that their life has value and purpose, and a child who does not. Our churches have a unique and God-given role to help form and shape the next generation. I pray that the ideas that you find in the following chapters will help you do just that.

Chapter 1 Reflection Questions

1. How does the brain learn?
2. How can I teach in a way that helps my students remember?
3. What can I do to ensure that I am not just planning and teaching a lesson that caters to the ways that I learn best? How can I reach the learning needs of all of my students?
4. What are some ways that I can build deeper relationships with the students I am working with?

2

Planning Lessons

"Pray that I may proclaim [the mystery of Christ] clearly, as I should." Colossians 4:4 NIV

SOME CHURCHES PURCHASE PRE-PACKAGED curricula and, in this case, the work of curriculum design is already basically finished. However, if this is not available to you or if you want to try something different, this chapter is designed to help you create your lessons and units from scratch.

Beginning questions–

1. What do you want to teach? Will it be based on a single biblical text (certain chapters or book of the Bible) or designed thematically based on a specific topic or idea?

2. How long will you be teaching it? (This might be a single 30 or 40-minute lesson, or a series of lessons taught over 6-10 weeks.) Consider how much time in minutes or hours you have to work with.

3. What are one or two focus questions that you can design your lesson or unit around? (For example, in Chapter 1, the first-grade lesson's focus question could have been, "What is

the kingdom of God like?" A unit for high schoolers could be built around the question, "What is God's purpose for my life?") Try to develop a focus question that is designed for big picture understanding—What do you want your students to remember 40 years from now about this topic or idea?

If you are designing an entire unit, you will need a calendar to start planning out the specifics of each week. The focus question may actually be the name of the study, like "What is God's purpose for my life?" or you can simplify it into a single word or phrase like "Purpose," or "Finding Purpose." The major focus question should remain the same throughout each week of the unit, but smaller guiding questions can be used for individual lessons. For example, accompanying weekly questions might be things like, "Does God really know me?" and "How can I grow in my relationship with God?"

No matter what type of a lesson you want to plan, or what the age groups are of the students with whom you are working, there are five things every lesson should include:

1. *Ice Breaker or Community-Building Beginning.* Always begin with something fun and conversational, even if it does not directly apply to the day's lesson. Some youth leaders I know start their lessons by having students share their highs and lows of the week. (This tends to work better in smaller settings.) An elementary Sunday school class might begin with sharing your favorite thing that happened that week or asking students to report on an "assignment" that you gave them from last week's lesson. This only needs to take a few minutes, but it helps establish a positive tone and encourages kids to be active participants in the group. Note: If you have an extra chatty group, you will need to restrict the time specifically so it does not cut too far into the regular lesson. It is okay if this beginning activity is not directly connected to the lesson. Community building is the focus.

2. *Hook.* This is where the more formal lesson begins. A lesson hook is a short opening to the lesson which takes between

3-5 minutes. It is a way to grab student attention and get them interested in what comes next in the lesson. Sometimes you might use a picture, story, or a short video clip as part of a hook. The goal here is that it is connected to the lesson content and increases engagement. The fishing reference is on purpose—what are you going to throw out into the water to make your school of fish interested enough to take the bait (or at least be interested in nibbling on it)? An effective hook is a powerful tool to get your students ready to think and learn!

3. *Conversation and Collaboration.* Learning always increases when students have opportunities to talk and share as part of the lesson. It is sometimes more difficult for quieter students to share in large groups, so break up the room into more manageable smaller groups when needed. This can be done quickly by having students turn and talk to one person sitting beside them. You can also have students move to groups of 3-5 to share. Project the discussion questions, write them on a whiteboard, or provide handouts so that they have something in writing to reference. It also helps if you give students a minute or two to think about the question before moving to groups so they do not feel put on the spot to come up with an answer too quickly. These questions can come at the beginning, middle, or end of a lesson, but make sure you build conversation and collaboration into every lesson.

4. *Ask Better Questions.* Real student learning is rarely passive. Saying, "Do you understand?" and getting a few head nods is not a way to tell if understanding has happened. What evidence do you have that students really "got it"? How do you know if there are any misconceptions because they misunderstood what you were saying? The best way to collect evidence of understanding in a group setting is to ask probing, thoughtful questions and provide time for replies. The best deeper-level questions are planned out ahead of time. Very few new pastors or youth workers are good at asking good questions without prior planning. (The good news is that you

will get better at it with practice!) Plan out a few questions that require higher-thinking levels and imbed them into the lesson. This is best done by including those questions on your lesson plan, handout, or slide projected on the wall so you do not have to remember them on the spot. Do a quick internet search on Bloom's taxonomy and/or Webb's Depth of Knowledge (DoK) to get an idea of different types of questions at different levels of understanding.

Wait time is also important after asking a question. Allowing sufficient processing time before you ask students to answer your questions will produce more thoughtful responses. Try to pause for at least ten seconds or more before soliciting an answer. The silence will be uncomfortable at first, but the results will be worth it!

5. *Check for Understanding.* There are two types of checking for understanding, one is based on directions, and the other is based on content. Checking for understanding based *on directions* involves asking a few questions to make sure that students are ready to begin an activity or task. Avoid yes/no answers. For example, "How many minutes do you have to work in your groups?" or, "What happens if you do not finish this worksheet today?" These may also include safety considerations like, "Why is it important not to get Expo markers on our clothes?" or, "Is anyone allergic to gluten?" Asking a few of these questions before the task begins will help maximize work time and spare you from repetitive questions in the middle of the project.

Checking for understanding *on content* usually comes at the end of a lesson or key idea. These are a few questions to make sure that students understand the heart of the lesson. Again, avoid yes/no answers whenever possible. "How might this topic make you look at the world differently this week?" or, "What part of our conversation today really stood out to you?" You could also very appropriately use the focus question for the unit or the guiding question for the lesson as a way to check for understanding as the lesson concludes.

PLANNING LESSONS

Now that we have established some lesson requirements, it is time to talk about actually planning a lesson. There are dozens of different instructional models out there to choose from, but in all of my years as an educator, I have found three models to be the most practical, and I have never found a lesson idea that would not fit within one of these three frameworks:

Direct Instruction—This model is most typically used when you are trying to teach a person or group how to do something or teach them about something in a shorter amount of time. The leader, teacher, or pastor holds the focus of the lesson. The leader walks the students through the steps of the lesson in an "I do, we do, you do" format. This method, often attributed to Madeline Hunter, is still the most commonly used in U.S. classrooms. However, it does not have to be boring drill and kill! Direct instruction can be very effective when used correctly and with a high-level of built-in student engagement.

Text-Based Reading—This model is designed for helping a class read through a Bible text together or watch some kind of informational video as a group. Many Sunday school lessons which focus on reading and discussing a specific chapter of the Bible can use this format. In this model, the text is the focus.

Inquiry—This type of lesson typically takes longer than the other two because students are collecting different types of information and drawing conclusions on their own. The teacher acts as a facilitator and "guide on the side." Studies have shown that inquiry learning helps students retain information the longest, but it is not necessarily suitable for every lesson that you teach. In this model, originally designed for science classrooms by Roger Bybee, the process of discovery learning is the focus.

Let's work through each of these types of lessons individually using the same topic so you can see how they function in similar and different ways. Remember that none of these models is necessarily better than the other. You just need to choose what is right for your style, the lesson itself, and the needs of your students. Variety is also important, so use different models on different days or weeks and see how it goes.

Direct Instruction Sample Lesson

Teacher's Role—Present the information and help students learn how to interpret it.

1. *Community Building* (4 minutes)

   Turn to the person next to you and share with them either the coolest building you have ever been in, or the coolest building you want to someday visit. After a few minutes of discussion, ask a few people to share their ideas with the whole group.

2. *Hook*—Get their attention (3 minutes)

   Project a few pictures of some modern-day buildings familiar to your students and have them guess how much each one cost to build. Then, project a picture of Solomon's temple. "We have been talking about the life of Solomon, and today we are going to talk about the temple that he built during his reign as king of Israel." How much do you think this cost to build?" After a few students guess, tell them it was not less than $30,000,000! "How long do you think it took to build?" After a few replies, tell them it took about seven years.

3. *Input*—Provide the important information your students need to know. Sometimes "Input" can be thought of as "I do" because I, as the instructor, am providing the necessary information. (15 minutes)

   Include the following information on slides that are projected or written on the board for students to see and talk about each item. Include a relevant picture on each slide.

Time Frame—According to 1 Kings, the foundation was laid in the second month of the fourth year of Solomon's reign and completed in the eighth month of his 11th year as king.

Workers—We know that there were at least 3,850 foremen and supervisors overseeing the project. Check for understanding: If there were that many overseers, how many total people might it have taken to build this temple? (We do not know the exact number, but it is good for students to wrestle with the sheer vastness of it all for a minute.)

Cedar from Lebanon—Hauled to the sea and floated in on rafts by Hiram, King of Tyre.

Continue on with slides which show other parts of the temple including depictions of the Ark of the Covenant, gold sheets with palm trees and cherubim, 10 golden lampstands, shewbread, altar of incense, etc.

Destruction—The temple was destroyed 400 years after it was built.

*Make sure to end this section by _____ (insert time here)

4. *Guided Practice*—Conversation /Collaboration, "We do" together (10 minutes)

Under your chairs you will each find a sticky note with one item from the temple. Walk around and find the other students who have the same item and sit in a group with them. Move the chairs as needed. As a group, answer the following questions (either projected or on a handout).

- What purpose do you think your item served in the temple? How heavy or expensive might it have been?
- Do you think God was glorified through the building of Solomon's temple? Why or why not?
- What are some things that we do today to glorify God, individually and collectively?

- Key Idea: 1 Corinthians 3:16 says that we are God's temple and God's spirit dwells in our midst. If we, today, think about ourselves as God's temple, how should that influence our decisions and the ways that we live? (Note that this question asks students to reflect collectively and is not as personal as an individual reflection at this point.)

5. *Independent Practice*—"You do" (10 minutes)

    Put your chairs back in rows and go back to your original seat.

    This week as you go home and to school, work, sports, or activities, think about what kinds of things bring God glory. If you are God's temple, what kind of a temple are you? What kinds of things can you do to bring God glory this week?

    If time is up, end here. As they are leaving, ask students to tell you or another volunteer one thing that they can do this week to bring God glory. If you still have a lot of time left, ask students to share ideas with the people sitting around them.

6. *Closure*—Wrap it up and preview, as time allows (3 minutes)

    Next week, we are going to talk about Solomon's palace, which took 13 years to build. Is there anything wrong with the fact that the temple took seven years to build and Solomon's palace took 13 years to build? As you leave today, tell me or another youth worker why this might be a problem.

Text-Based Reading Sample Lesson

Teacher's Role—Walk students through a text and make sure that they understand what they are reading by planning before, during, and after reading activities. In this model, the text provides the primary information, not the instructor. Note that some of the lesson elements can be the same, but the core focus is different.

PLANNING LESSONS

1. *Community Building* (4 minutes)

    Turn to the person next to you and share with them either the coolest building you have ever been in, or the coolest building you want to someday visit. After a few minutes of discussion, ask a few people to share their ideas with the whole group.

2. *Hook*—Get their attention (3 minutes)

    Project a few pictures of some modern-day buildings familiar to your students and have them guess how much each one cost to build. Then, project a picture of Solomon's temple. "We have been talking about the life of Solomon, and today we are going to talk about the temple that he built during his reign as king of Israel." How much do you think this cost to build?" After a few students guess, tell them it was not less than $30,000,000! "How long do you think it took to build?" After a few replies, tell them it took about seven years.

3. *Before Reading*—Review previous learning or build the background needed to understand the lesson (5 minutes)

    Let's remember together what we have been studying in this unit. Which of David's sons became king after David died? David wanted to build a temple for God, but God told him he could not. Turn to a partner and discuss why God did not want David to build the temple. Why was Solomon a better choice? (A few minutes later) Personal connection: Are there any things that your parents want you to do that they were not able to do themselves? (Consider sharing a quick personal story here.) Have students turn to a partner and give an example if they have something that applies.

4. *During Reading*—Conversation/Collaboration. Stop at designated places to check for understanding and prepare students for the next passage. (20 minutes)

    Under your chairs you will each find a sticky note with one item from Solomon's temple. Walk around and find the other students who have the same item and sit in a group with them. Move the chairs as needed.

We are going to read 1 Kings 6 today and learn about how Solomon constructed the temple. (Depending on the reading level and preferences of your students, read these passages aloud to them, or ask volunteers in the small groups to read each section.) As they come to the end of a section, groups should answer the accompanying questions before moving on.

Write on the board for reference: 1 cubit = about 18 inches (the length from the elbow to the tip of the middle finger) You could even have students practice measuring how tall they are in cubits if you have extra time.

Passage #1—1 Kings 6:1-13

- How big was Solomon's temple? Estimate the approximate length and height. As a group, use your elbows and arms to demonstrate about the size of one of the lowest side rooms.
- What promise did God give to Solomon as he was building the temple? Why was this important?

Now that we know about how big the temple was, we are going to read about how they designed the inside. This is a longer passage, so as we read, try to visualize what some of these objects might have looked like.

Passage #2—1 Kings 6:14-38

- What items in the temple were made out of gold? List several of them.
- How big were the cherubim? What might your reaction have been if you saw one of these statues?
- Why is it important that the Bible gives us such a detailed description of the building of the temple?

5. *After Reading*—Build further comprehension or knowledge by bringing it all together. Focus on the big ideas you want them to remember. (5 minutes)

Students remain in groups. Share with them in conclusion that 1 Corinthians 3:16 says that we are God's temple and God's spirit dwells in our midst. (Project verse if possible.) If we, today, think about ourselves as God's temple, how should that influence our decisions and the ways that we live?

This week as you go home and to school, work, sports, or activities, think about what kinds of things bring God glory. If you are God's temple, what kind of a temple are you? What kinds of things can you do to bring God glory this week?

If time is up, end here. As they are leaving, ask students to tell you or another volunteer one thing that they can do this week to bring God glory. If you still have a lot of time left, ask students to share ideas with the people sitting around them.

*Make sure to end this section by _____ (insert time here)

6. *Closure*—Wrap it up and preview, as time allows. (3 minutes)

Next week we are going to talk about Solomon's palace, which took 13 years to build. Is there anything wrong with the fact that the temple took seven years to build and Solomon's palace took 13 years to build? As you leave today, tell me or another youth worker why this might be a problem.

Inquiry Sample Lesson

Teacher's Role—Facilitate the learning as a "guide on the side." Allow students to find the answers and make connections primarily on their own. While it is important to clarify misconceptions, the goal is for students to be the primary investigators.

1. *Community Building* (4 minutes)

   Turn to the person next to you and share with them either the coolest building you have ever been in, or the coolest building you want to someday visit. After a few minutes of discussion, ask a few people to share their ideas with the whole group.

2. *Hook/Engage*—Get their attention by engaging their curiosity. Start with an interesting question that the class explores as a group. (3 minutes)

   Project a few pictures of some modern-day buildings familiar to your students and have them guess how much each one cost to build. Then, project a picture of Solomon's temple. "We have been talking about the life of Solomon, and today we are going to talk about the temple that he built during his reign as king of Israel." How much do you think this cost to build?" After a few students guess, tell them it was not less than $30,000,000! "How long do you think it took to build?" After a few replies, tell them it took about seven years.

3. *Explore/Explain*—Students take on the role of researchers. They are encouraged to make their own connections and conclusions. (20 minutes)

   Today, I want you to act like archeologists. A recent archeological dig has uncovered some ancient artifacts that may have been housed in Solomon's temple. Your job is to examine the artifact or picture of the artifact and see if it is mentioned in 1 Kings 6-7.

   You can choose to work in groups of two, three, or four. I am going to give you a minute to find a group to work with. Now, I am handing out a piece of paper with 10 items listed. You have the next 20 minutes to go around the room and look at these 10 items or pictures of an item at each station. If you think that this is something that could have been in the temple, list your rationale on the worksheet. See if you can find the Bible reference in 1 Kings to support your answer.

(It is okay to include a few items that were not there, for the sake of inquiry, to help them really think about what they are reading, like a hammer or silver chain.)

4. *Evaluate*—What will students do with what they have learned? How will you know that they really understand the key ideas? (10 minutes)

Once groups have moved around to the 10 stations, they should return to their seats, but still sit in groups. (You will know everyone is done once they are all seated.) Groups should discuss the following questions:

- How does exploring these artifacts help you better understand what the temple might have looked like?
- Do you think God was glorified through the building of Solomon's temple? Why or why not?
- What are some things that we do today to glorify God, individually and collectively?
- Key Idea: 1 Corinthians 3:16 says that we are God's temple and God's spirit dwells in our midst. If we, today, think about ourselves as God's temple, how should that influence our decisions and the ways that we live? (Note that this question asks students to reflect collectively and is not as personal as an individual reflection at this point.)

*Make sure to end this section by _____ (insert time here)

5. *Extend*—How can students apply these ideas to new or more personal situations? (4 minutes)

This week, as you go home and to school, work, sports, or activities, think about what kinds of things bring God glory. If you are God's temple, what kind of a temple are you? What kinds of things can you do to bring God glory this week?

If time is up, end here. As they are leaving, ask students to tell you or another volunteer one thing that they can do this week to bring God glory. If you still have a lot of time left, ask students to share ideas with the people sitting around them.

6. *Closure*—Wrap it up and preview, as time allows (3 minutes)

Next week we are going to talk about Solomon's palace, which took 13 years to build. Is there anything wrong with the fact that the temple took seven years to build and Solomon's palace took 13 years to build? As you leave today, tell me or another youth worker why this might be a problem.

As you can see, in each of these lesson plans, there are several ways that you can get to the same big idea understanding without having every lesson following the exact same pattern. I hope that experimenting with these three different types of models will give you some ways to add variety and creativity to your teaching and lesson design.

Time Considerations

One of the most difficult things to gauge when you are new to the planning process is how long things will take. It is always best to over plan, with more than enough material, and then determine ahead of time what you will cut if needed. Look at each of the lesson elements. Plan out how long you think each section will take, then have an adjustment plan ready if needed. Often the best part of the lesson comes at the end, but if you are running short on time, this can get squeezed out or minimized. Therefore, it can be helpful to have a specific time listed. For example, in your lesson plan, you can say by 10:15 a.m. you need to be at a certain place in the lesson to allow enough time to finish with a powerful conclusion.

It is also helpful to allow the last five minutes of a lesson for cleanup and looking ahead. For little ones, this might be time to clean up materials from the lesson and straighten chairs or carpet squares so the room is ready for the next group or lesson. For older kids, this could be a time when you preview what is coming in the following weeks or leave time for prayer requests or random Bible questions that they might have. I have found that having a more low-key end to a lesson provides students with time to think, process and continue to build community. It also helps your student with anxiety not worry about getting to the main church service on time after Sunday school, or not worry that an older sibling is impatiently waiting in the parking lot to drive them home after Wednesday night activities.

Group Configurations

As students get older, they tend to sit with the same people and gravitate toward others with similar likes and interests. In many ways, this is human nature, and as adults we do the same thing! In church settings, we want students to be comfortable enough that they are willing to participate, but not so comfortable that they stop reaching out to others who are new or different. Again, variety is important here. Try to alternate between free-choice groupings and mixing up your groups as often as possible to help students get to know others better.

Here are a few fun ideas to get students into groups:

1. Color cards—Place colored post-it notes on the underside of chairs.
2. Birthdays—Ask students to line up according to birthdays. Then divide the long line into as many smaller groups as you need.
3. Seasons—Have students move to one of the four corners of the room based either on their most or least favorite season.
4. Candy—Have students each pick a starburst or another individually wrapped colored candy as they enter the room. Then have them get into groups based on the types of candy or color of wrapper that they chose.
5. Pairs—As students enter the room, give them a card with one item listed. Then, have them wander around the room

and find a connected item (sun and moon, apple and orange, river and lake, nickel and dime, etc.). These two people then become partners for the next activity. When appropriate, it is also fun to connect the pairings to things you have been studying (Adam and Eve, David and Bathsheba, Priscilla and Aquila, etc.).

6. Playing cards—Hand out a deck of cards, with each student receiving one card. Depending on the size of group you need, students then group themselves in one of several ways—suits, face cards, numbers, etc.

7. Clothing—This is harder to plan ahead, because you do not know what your students will be wearing, but use their articles of clothing to help sort into groups. (E.g.: everyone with short sleeves move to this side, if you have long sleeves move to this side; if you are wearing sandals go to the back of the room, if you have other types of shoes move to the front; if you have any kind of jewelry on, go to the left, if you are not wearing any jewelry, go to the right, etc.)

Knowing Your Students

Our natural inclination is to teach the way that we have been taught, or teach the way that we like to learn. It is important to remember that not all of your students will have similar backgrounds, passions, or learning styles as you do. As you get to know the students that you are working with, it will become easier to plan because you can find ways to tailor your lessons to match their interests and the ways that they learn best. So, how can you determine how best to teach and connect with your students? Ask them!

Informal conversations with children and teens about the types of things they do in their free time, what classes they like best at school, or how they like to have information presented can garner helpful information. You might also consider developing an information sheet that students fill out for you and your church at the beginning of every school year. Keep some extra copies for students who come as visitors or transfer to your area in the middle of the year. The following are some helpful items and questions that you may want to use in developing a student information sheet for your children's program or youth group. (Some questions are age-specific, so use what works for your setting and the ages of your students.)

> Full Name:
>
> Nickname or name you preferred to be called by:
>
> Birthdate:
>
> Your phone number:
>
> Your parent/guardian's phone number (if different):
>
> Email:
>
> Who do you live with?
>
> Who usually brings you to church?
>
> How do you describe yourself? Circle all that apply.
>
> > artistic, athletic, studious, adventurous, thoughtful or _____ (your word here)
>
> What are some of your hobbies?
>
> What is your favorite subject in school?
>
> What clubs, activities, or sports are you involved in at school?
>
> What is your favorite food?
>
> What is your favorite kind of pizza?
>
> What is your favorite kind of donut?
>
> What are you allergic to?
>
> What are some of your pet peeves?
>
> What are some of your favorite college or professional sports teams?
>
> Where is one place you would like to travel?

Describe what you would consider to be your perfect day . . .

What is one question you have about God?

Is there anything else you want us to know about you?

Chapter 2 Reflection Questions

1. What are the most important ideas to remember when planning a lesson?
2. How can I capture and keep the attention of my students?
3. Of the five things that every lesson should include, what area is the easiest to implement? What aspect will be the most challenging for me?
4. What are the ideas or concepts that I most want my students to remember 40 years from now? How can I teach so that these ideas are always at the forefront?
5. What is one thing I can do this week to get to know my students better?

3

Managing Behaviors

"In your relationships with one another, have the same mindset as Christ Jesus." Philippians 2:5 NIV

Every teacher education program includes at least one course on classroom management, and it is no wonder! Misbehavior, disruptive outbursts, and getting and keeping student focus for extended periods of time is exhausting and a typical reason why many teachers burn out. It becomes even more challenging in a church setting because students are choosing to be there, so there are not the typical consequences of bad grades or detention to use as motivators. We want students to love church activities and truly have fun being there, so what can pastors and volunteers do to keep students engaged and on task while not coming across as drill sergeants?

As we discussed in the last chapter, planning for the content of a successful lesson takes some work ahead of time. In the same way, behavior management takes planning. The old adage is still true—students will rise to the expectations you set for them. It is important to state here that sometimes there are cognitive issues or emotional disturbances that can get in the way of student learning. We will discuss strategies for individual outlier situations in subsequent chapters. This chapter is designed to give you ideas on strategies for group behavior management as you work with groups of students either on a weekly basis or for special events like Vacation Bible School or church camp.

It is first important to consider some guiding principles upon which we base our expectations. If you walk into any traditional school classroom, you will likely see classroom or school rules posted. This can be an effective model to follow, and we can base our written and spoken expectations on biblical principles...

1. Love God and Love Others. Matthew 22:37-40
2. Be Kind to Each Other. Romans 12:10
3. Shine Your Light. Matthew 5:16
4. Be a Good Listener. James 1:19
5. Honor and Respect Your Leaders. Hebrews 13:17

... And so many more!

In all of my work with student teachers, there are usually two reasons why a lesson fails. The first is poor planning for the content and delivery of the lesson. The second is that behavioral expectations were not clearly stated up front. What does that mean, exactly? Just like you have to plan for the content of a lesson, you also need to plan for the desired behaviors you want to see in each part of the lesson. Students need to know your expectations for things like the volume level of a discussion, whether or not hands have to be raised to answer a question, and if it is okay if they move around the room or use the restroom without permission.

So, what is appropriate behavior for your setting? That is what you need to decide beforehand based on your setting, your style, and the needs of your students. If you remember back to your own school days as a student, you may have had some teachers who were very strict and some who were very lenient. Expectations for behavior changed each time the bell rang and you went into a different classroom. This can be very confusing for students because what is okay in one classroom is not okay in the next. They will wander into church on Sunday morning and Wednesday nights having no idea what to expect. When you have planned ahead of time what behaviors you want to see, then you can effectively communicate your expectations to them and take the guesswork and stress out of coming to church.

As you look at your lesson plan, identify all of the different components of the lesson. Remember that planning for both content *and* behavior at every stage is the magic combination! Consider each of the following and determine your expectations.

1. *Entrances and Exits*—What should students do as they enter the room? If they are coming from Sunday school to children's church, do they immediately go to their seats, or do they have time to play and interact casually first? If it is a Wednesday night activity, and students can arrive at different times, what might you do for the first few minutes so latecomers do not miss too much?

2. *Interactions*—How many places in the lesson have you planned for collaborative or conversation time? Will students choose their own groups or partners, or will you do it for them? (If so, how will you do this?) How will you make sure that no students are left out? As students talk in groups, what is the expected noise level? What can you build into the directions to make sure that all students have the chance to share and no one dominates the conversation or is ignored?

3. *Distribution of Materials*—Carefully think through all of the necessary supplies for the lesson ahead of time and determine how they will be distributed. Should students pick up a handout as they enter the room or are you going to have someone pass them out? Can the students take one and pass it down the row, or does someone need to individually hand out each item? At the elementary levels especially, students love to be the classroom helpers. You might have one volunteer hand out Bibles, one pass out markers, and one or two stack the carpet squares at the end of the lesson. The more

responsibilities you can give your students, the more invested they will be in the process and the community.

4. *Cell Phones*—As students get older, they are more likely to bring a phone or personal device with them to church. This presents some great opportunities to do web searches, use the Bible App, record funny skits, and market your youth program by the pictures the students post. However, they can also be a distraction if students just want to sit in the back and play games or check out of the real community around them as they scan social media. Establish your rules for phone use. Are there times when it is okay that they are out, and other times when they need to be put away and on silent mode? Make sure your expectations are clear and remember that you may need to state them each week! Helping students understand the reasons behind the rules also helps them understand why those rules are important. (Note: Consistency is important here. If you do not want your students to have phones out, then your youth workers should not have theirs out either.)

5. *Transitions*—Moving from one activity to the next, taking a group bathroom break, or filling time while you wait for the main church service to end can be some of the most discipline-prone times of the entire lesson. Identify the transitions in the lesson and have a plan for how you will approach each one. Remember that transitions can be fun—"Can we all tiptoe as quietly as we can to the door?" Or, "Last time we cleaned up in 50 seconds, do you think we can be faster this time?" It is also very appropriate to have students help you clean up and reset the room when needed. This also helps them have ownership in the space that is theirs.

6. *Leadership Development*—As students get older, giving them opportunities to develop leadership skills can be very empowering and help them find a way to belong. How might you establish a leadership council or advisory team to help you plan lessons, activities, and outings? Stay away from the

traditional President, Vice President, etc. roles, and think more about things like communications manager, greeters, visitor outreach, event photographers, and other roles that students can move in and out of as their time allows. One of our kids' favorite days was when the older members of the youth group welcomed them by writing fun messages on our home driveway in chalk and waking them up early one Saturday morning to take them to breakfast. These simple things made them so excited to be part of the youth group!

Now that you have a plan for each of these items, the key is to communicate the plan effectively to students. As you explain directions, include your expectations for noise level, movement, participation, etc. Determining your behavioral expectations and stating them clearly will help reduce the majority of your discipline issues. Expectations should be stated each time you begin a new activity. Also remember to check for understanding to make sure that they have clearly understood the plan!

The One-Minute Rule

So, how long should I expect my students to pay attention? While I have never found a specific research study which answers this question definitively, especially considering the variety of learners that exist, all of my experience in the classroom has led me to preach what I call the one-minute rule. On average, I have found that people can really pay attention for about one minute for every year that they are old. A typical five-year old can pay attention for about five minutes before he or she becomes distracted or wants to do something else. A ten-year old has about a ten-minute attention span. This means that if I am working primarily with ten-year olds, every ten minutes in the lesson we need to mix things up and bring in a new activity or discussion. It would be wrong for me to think that an eight-year old could pay attention as long as an 18-year old can! If I time my lessons to fit the appropriate attention spans of the students that I am working with, there will be less chance of behavioral issues because we will transition to something different before they lose interest. (By the way, I think that this rule peaks at about 20-25 minutes. Most adults can't focus on something longer than about that time unless they are really interested. Keep this in mind if you are planning a sermon!)

Planning for Engagement

When students are having fun and are interested in the content, they are much more likely to participate. If they have to sit and listen to someone talk for too long, they are much more likely to fall asleep, fidget, or exhibit attention-seeking behaviors. One of the best discipline plans is a great lesson plan, so plan for engagement as much as possible throughout the lesson. The following are some easy ways to do this:

- Object lessons
- Role playing
- Scenarios
- Visuals
- Games
- Interaction/questioning
- Short video clips
- Hand motions
- Funny questions or jokes
- Songs
- Costumes or props
- Funny noises
- Intentionally telling the story incorrectly and having them correct it
- Charades
- Short, personal stories

Getting Attention

Every master teacher has some sort of attention-getting tool in their arsenal. Raising your voice or "shushing" students is rarely effective in the long run. Think instead about quick and fun ways that you can draw their focus back to you. At first, you may want to experiment with different ideas and see what works best for you, your setting, and the kids you are working with. You will want to rehearse these and explicitly teach them to students so that they know what you expect and how it might be used. Here are some ideas:

- Giant timer projected in front
- Verbal countdown 5-4-3-2-1
- "If you can hear me, put your finger on your nose. If you can hear me, put your finger on your ear . . . " and so on until everyone is listening and participating
- Give me five. Put your hand up and wait for every student to put up their hand too (you can also use this as a countdown device with your fingers)
- Flickering the lights (this may be a trigger for kids with trauma in their backgrounds, so use with caution)
- Call and response with funny sayings or biblical duos (I say Adam, you say Eve.)
- A chime, gong, or other sound effect
- Clap once, students respond by clapping twice
- Clap in a fun rhythm/sequence and have students repeat you; this can be done several times until all are participating

My brother taught third grade for many years before moving up to the middle-school level. He told me it was easy to get his students to look at anything but the teacher, so he used that and developed a strategy when he needed all eyes on him. He picked a few different things in the room and would say, "Okay students, everyone close your mouths and look at the *clock*; now everyone look at the *bookshelf;* now everyone look at me." He chose different things each time, so there was a lot of variety, but just the act of everyone looking at different things first and then focusing back on the teacher worked like magic every time.

If some of the things on the list seem too silly or juvenile for the level of kids you are working with, find something that works for you and that you can be comfortable using on a regular basis. It will feel a little awkward at first, but after a few times both you and your students will get into the routine, which will help you more effectively manage your group.

Use Proximity

While most senior pastors tend to preach from behind a podium or pulpit on Sunday mornings, it is much more effective in children's church or youth group if the speaker is moving around the room during the message or lesson. This will help you connect with different groups of kids and they tend to be more alert if they have to watch you from different parts of the room. Try to stay on the perimeter as you move around (as opposed to going up and down aisles too often) because this allows you to see the greatest majority of the students at the same time and they will not only see the back of your head. This also discourages misbehaviors from the back rows!

If you do have a student or group of students who tend to be off-task, one of the first steps is to simply move closer to them. You could assign a volunteer to sit in this group specifically, or simply wander over to their location as you are talking to the whole group and stay in their general area. Most of the time the undesirable behavior will stop if there is an adult close by. If you move to a different location and the talking continues or cell phones come back out, simply move back over into that area again.

Your Bored Face

Warning: Your smile may reinforce the wrong behaviors! Early on in my teaching career, an observer pointed out to me that a group of boys were misbehaving in the back of the room and when I looked over at them, I smiled.

"Yes, and?" I replied. I smile a lot, so this was not a surprising observation.

My coach replied, "When you just smiled at that group, it gave them permission to continue the off-task behavior. Your smile told them what they were doing was okay."

I was astounded by that statement. My smile was actually working against me as a management technique! The more I thought about it, the more I knew it was true. I had to learn to more closely monitor my facial expressions and body language in the ways that I responded to misbehavior.

So where should you start? It might be very helpful to have a coach, like I did, observe a lesson and note (in writing) the ways that you respond to students, both positively and negatively. It will give you some very helpful feedback! Another very practical thing that you can rehearse is looking in the mirror and developing a "bored" face (if you do not have one already). It is a look that is very effective when you want students to know that you see what they are doing and it needs to stop. A bored face is not a mean face; it is simply a response which says to students, "Really? This is silly. You can be better than this." As I have perfected my bored face, it also includes raising an eyebrow or two. If you are trying to discourage off-task behaviors, start with proximity and a bored face.

Escalations

If the behavior issues continue after you have tried the things previously mentioned, then things get more serious. You may need to separate students to other corners of the room. Some students may need a physical cooling off time when they go to a quiet place for a few minutes. Other students may need to take a walk and talk with an adult about what is bothering them. As you get to know your students better, it is very appropriate to talk with them and their parents about what works best for them when they are angry or frustrated. (This is more effectively done not in the heat of the moment, but later after they have de-escalated.)

Whenever you have a student that is irate, for whatever reason, it is important to monitor your physical demeanor. Directly facing a student and looking them in the eye can be considered aggressive and may actually escalate the behavior. Instead, stand or sit beside the student so you are shoulder to shoulder instead of face to face—this brings more of a friend-to-friend approach instead and will de-escalate the behavior more quickly. Additionally, do not respond with a loud voice or demands. Instead, quietly seek to understand what is wrong and what the student most needs right in the moment. Some students may need someone to verbally process with them what they are feeling, and others may just need space to collect themselves before they have to answer too many questions. Helpful responses might include: "I am ready to take a walk with you whenever you are ready to talk," or "Why don't you go get a drink and take a minute by yourself?" As quickly as you can, redirect the rest of the group so that they have something else to work on and are not just staring at the student who is struggling.

In extreme situations, discipline plans may need to be in place, especially if the child or teen has the potential of hurting themselves or others. Usually, if extreme behaviors happen at church, they are also happening at school. It is very appropriate to talk with parents or guardians about behavior plans that are in place at school. Here are some questions you can ask regarding behavior plans:

- What is effective?
- What are some triggers that may make the student respond more aggressively?
- What safety plan is in place if the student needs to go home because they are not able to settle down?

- What needs to happen before the student is allowed to return to regular church activities?

While these conversations are very difficult, they are very important for the safety and well-being of everyone in your program.

Cooling Off

Being aware of your own emotions and limitations is an important part of being an effective pastor or volunteer. Crafty (and hurting) kids quickly learn how to push your buttons and there will be a few who want to see just how far they can push you. Remaining calm and collected is paramount, even when the situations are stressful. It is important to have a plan for what you will do when you feel your face getting redder or your blood pressure rising due to student behaviors.

There are many fast and simple breathing techniques which can help lower anxiety and help clear your head quickly so you can go on with your work with students. One of my favorites is the 4-7-8 breathing technique. Breathe in for four seconds, hold your breath for seven seconds, and exhale for eight seconds. If you do not already have a go-to technique or plan for what you can do in the moment to regain control, explore some options this week. Controlling our emotions is an important thing to model for students, and in the process, you can encourage them to find some of their own ways to self-regulate when it becomes necessary.

Shifting Gears

In any ministry setting, there are fun surprises (treats, special guests, a wacky wig worn by the youth pastor) and not-so-fun surprises, like when play time or an engaging activity ends and students are not ready for the amusement to stop. It is important to have a plan in place for those times when your group needs to transition from something wild and crazy to something more serious. A transition time is needed to prepare them to calm down or start thinking more seriously. Very few children and teens are ready to transition at the flip of a switch, so have a plan ready to help them shift gears. For example, late nights in the cabin at church camp or a youth retreat can be rough because the kids want to stay up and the counselor is exhausted and desperately needs sleep. Plan a gradual shift in energy which is less abrupt and gets you out of the "bad guy" role, demanding everyone goes to sleep. After devotions and prayer time is finished, allow the campers to talk quietly with room lights off and flashlights on for five minutes. At the end of five minutes, the talking has to stop, but the flashlights can stay on for another five minutes. At the end of that time, all lights are off and there is no talking. This 10-minute transition provides a progression for students to slowly wind down and settle in. The same is true of play or free time between Sunday school and kids' church. Project a giant timer and give a verbal countdown so they know when it is time to return to their seats and be ready to listen.

These simple planning tools help eliminate surprises and will strengthen your relationship with students because they will begin to trust you to prepare them for what is coming next.

Never Alone

In every children's or youth program, there will inevitably be students with whom you connect with more quickly and those that are more difficult to reach. It is incredibly important that you care about all of your kids, even those that drive you crazy sometimes. Church workers are not superhuman, and there will be days when you are tired and frustrated from things happening at home, work, or church. No matter what your day or week has been like prior to coming to church, God will give you the strength you need for the moment. It is always within our reach, but we need to ask for it. Those quick prayers for help and guidance in the car or as you walk into the youth room connect us with the Creator of the Universe, who intimately knows us and our students. There is freedom and renewal when we place everything in God's hands and ask

God for the strength to reach the children and teens that we will be interacting with that day.

Jeremiah 33:3 is an important verse to remember as you are preparing to work with the kids that God has placed under your guidance. "Call to me and I will answer you and tell you great and unsearchable things you do not know." You do not know what that upcoming lesson or event is going to hold, but God does, and you can rest in the fact that God will be right there with you through every moment.

Chapter 3 Reflection Questions

1. What should I do with inattentive or disruptive students?
2. How can I stay positive and focused?
3. In what areas do I feel I am able to be clearest in stating my expectations? In what areas do I need to be clearer?
4. How can I effectively address the use of cell phones, headphones, or *[insert another distraction here]* during whole or small group times together?
5. What do I know works with the students I have now? What is not working?
6. How might our team be able to utilize classroom teachers or other professionals in our congregation for coaching and ideas about managing specific behaviors?

4

IEPs and 504 Plans

"If you need wisdom, ask our generous God, and He will give it to you. He will not rebuke you for asking." James 1:5 NLT

IT WILL ONLY TAKE about five minutes with a group of students at church to catch a glimpse of how uniquely God created each one of them. Within that diverse group, it is very likely that some of the students in your children's program or youth group will have some special needs that may interfere with their learning or the ways in which they interact with others. This chapter is designed to give you some basic training on special education in schools which may have helpful implications and applications to you and your team in a church setting.

It was not until the 1970's in the United States that advocates and parents used new state laws and litigation to champion federal legislation and funding to assist in the education of students with disabilities. In 1975, the Education for All Handicapped Children Act (also known as Public Law 94-142) passed. The original legislation went through several reauthorizations, and in 1990, it was renamed the Individuals with Disabilities Education Act (IDEA).[1]

---

1. Individuals with Disabilities Education Act, 2010.

These federal laws mandate that all students with disabilities between the ages of three and 21 in the U.S. are eligible to receive a "free, appropriate public education" (FAPE). IDEA requires that students must be placed in a setting which allows maximum contact with non-disabled peers, usually the regular education classroom, while still having their special learning needs met. This setting is usually referred to as the Least Restrictive Environment (LRE).[2] IDEA also requires that related services like transportation, psychological treatment, specific therapies, and other related assistance be provided by the school when necessary to help the student have access to education.

All public k-12 schools are required to have a process in place to identify and evaluate students suspected of having a disability to determine if they are eligible to receive special services beyond what is provided to students in the general education population. IDEA (2010) defines a child with a disability as meeting at least one of the following 13 categories:

> Having an intellectual disability, a hearing impairment (including deafness), a speech or language impairment, a visual impairment (including blindness), a serious emotional disturbance, an orthopedic impairment, autism, traumatic brain injury, other health impairment, a specific learning disability, deaf-blindness, or multiple disabilities, and who, by reason thereof, needs special education and related services. (Section 300.8a1)

Before a student can receive services, a multidisciplinary team must complete a comprehensive evaluation of the student's needs. As part of the process, they may consider assessment and evidence from the following areas: educational, medical, social historical, psychological, or any other relevant area specific to the student.[3] If the student is found eligible for special education services under IDEA, then the team determines what services and interventions best meet the needs of the student in a school

---

2. Martin, "The Legislative and Litigation History of Special Education." 34-36.

3. Anderson, *Negotiating the Special Education Maze*, 47-49.

setting. In order to be eligible for special education, a specific diagnosis is required, but it is the specific learning needs, not the disability label, which determines what a typical day in the classroom will look like for that student.

Individualized Education Plans (IEPs)

Students in public k-12 schools who qualify for special education are required to have an IEP that is personalized and IDEA compliant. These are typically written by the special education teacher or program director and are required to be reviewed annually by the IEP team and re-evaluated every three years. IDEA requires the following information be included in the IEP:

- Statement of the student's level(s) of functioning and how the disability affects involvement in the general education program
- Current levels of educational performance
- Extent to which the student can participate in state-mandated assessments
- Specific reference to any behavioral issue(s) and strategies to address behavioral needs
- Determination of the least restrictive environment for the student
- Measurable annual and long-term goals
- Transition services for work or post-secondary education for students 16 years old or older

Typical IEP teams will include some of the following professionals: the special education teacher and/or director, school nurse, school psychologist, occupational therapist, physical therapist, speech-language pathologist, regular education teacher(s), and the school counselor. As students get older, it is best practice for them to participate in their own IEP meetings as well. Parents are also a very important part of this team, and they are welcome to invite any other participants that they chose. Depending on your relationship with the family, it would be very appropriate for a youth or children's pastor to attend the annual meeting if invited by the parents or student. You will learn a lot about what is happening with the student at school and what types of things are working and what is not in group educational settings. It is important to note that while churches are entirely separate from the public-school setting and are in no way required to follow accommodations or provide services like schools are, an IEP can still be a helpful reference for you. This can help you not only get to know the student's needs outside of church, but it may also give you some really good insights about how you might better serve and assist the student *at* church.

Parents will receive a paper or digital copy of their student's IEP each year. This is usually considered a confidential document within the school system, but parents are able to share their copy with whomever they wish. Whether or not you are able to attend the meeting, it may also be helpful for you to ask the parent or guardian if they are willing to share their copy of the IEP with you so you can get some ideas on ways to better help the student at church. Don't be surprised if parents are a little startled by this request, because it is not usually part of normal church conversations. However, it will reinforce your desire to be part of the student's circle of support not only on Wednesday nights and Sunday mornings, but throughout all aspects of their life.

IEPs are specific to k-12 public school settings and the services and accommodations for that student end once they graduate from high school. Legally, students who qualify for special education are able in most states to attend a public high school until the semester in which they turn 21. Most schools provide some sort of transition services for students aged 18-21 to better equip them with life skills including cooking, shopping, money management, etc.

504 Plans

Whereas IEPs are documents specific to students in special education programs, 504 Plans are for qualifying students in the general education program at a public school. (Remember that private school or homeschool students probably will not have these documents.) 504 Plans get their name from Section 504 of the Rehabilitation Act of 1973, a civil-rights statute designed to prohibit discrimination for individuals on the basis of a disability in activities or programs receiving federal funding.[4] These obligations are applicable to public schools, but the Americans with Disabilities Act of 1990 and Americans with Disabilities Amendments Act of 2008 further extend this protection to include a range of state and local government services and programs, including public schools, even if they do not receive any federal financial assistance. Unlike IEPs, protections under Section 504 can continue to college and beyond for individuals.

To be protected under Section 504, a student who attends a public school must meet the following criteria:

1. Have a physical or mental impairment which substantially limits one or more major life areas;
2. Have a record of such an impairment; or
3. Be regarded as having such an impairment

Public schools are required by law to provide a free appropriate public education (FAPE) to identified students with physical or mental impairments that substantially limit one or more major life activities. These life activities may include (but are not limited to) walking, hearing, seeing, speaking, eating, caring for one's self, working, and, most commonly used in schools—learning.

Common qualifying conditions for 504 Plans in schools are dyslexia, learning disorders, ADHD, epilepsy, visual impairments, emotional illnesses, etc. Usually they are not temporary conditions, but technically a temporary 504 Plan can be written

---

4. Section 504, Rehabilitation Act, 1973.

for a short-term disability like a broken leg or surgery recovery which lasts only a few months. Most of the time, however, the impairment is permanent or lasting and something that the student usually does not outgrow.

A food aversion, like disliking peanut butter, may be inconvenient, but it does not substantially limit a major life area and is not considered a disability. However, a severe food allergy, such as a peanut allergy, may be considered a disability because an allergic reaction significantly impacts the major life areas of eating and breathing.

One of the key ideas behind Section 504 is that students with significant disabilities may need additional support to be successful in school and should not experience discrimination on the basis of their disability. These accommodations should be specific to the student and can range from extended time on tests to permission to bring and store medical equipment (i.e. needles and insulin).[5]

504 Plans are created by a team who is assembled to determine eligibility. This group typically includes the school counselor, parent or guardian, student (when appropriate), and some of the current classroom teachers in the subject(s) where the disability is most manifested. Since this is outside of special education, it is usually the school counselor who takes the lead on creating and maintaining a 504 Plan. Just like an IEP, parents can bring additional guests with them to the meeting if they desire.

While the law does not provide a specific timeline for renewal of this document, best practice is to review the 504 Plan every year and re-evaluate every three years. All classroom teachers for that student should be provided with the 504 at the beginning of the year and are required by law to follow the listed accommodations. A 504 Plan is usually much shorter than an IEP, and is typically only a one or two-page document.

Just like an IEP, it may be helpful for pastors and church volunteers to have a copy of a student's 504 plan or at least be aware of the issue which was used to qualify the student for the plan. Many accommodations listed on the document are very practical

5. Yell, *The Law and Special Education*, 93-126.

and can be applied in a variety of settings—for example, a verbal prompt, preferential seating, frequent breaks, or even allowing the student to leave a few minutes early to get down or up the stairs before they get too busy during a transition.

Keep in mind that a student does not have to have a 504 Plan for you to offer an accommodation to them. Good teaching and behavior management practices are helpful for all students, even if you do not have any students in the room with specific disabilities. Laws also do not require that churches abide by accommodations which may be required in school settings. However, consistent practices between church, home, and school may help the student feel more welcome and less anxious about expectations in your Sunday school room or youth group.

As this chapter concludes, what do you need to remember? IEPs and 504 plans for students contain qualifying conditions, helpful accommodations, goals and/or strategies to increase learning, and the identification of a school-based support team. As part of the student's support team at church, it may be helpful for you to be aware of or participate in the conversations about the student's needs at school so you can better understand how the church can also effectively reach and address the learning needs of these individuals.

Chapter 4 Reflection Questions

1. What is the difference between an IEP and a 504?
2. What types of special needs do the students in my group currently have?
3. How is the information in this chapter useful if some of my students are homeschooled?
4. How might our church work with our local school to better assist our students with special needs?

5

Autism and ADHD

"But those who trust in the Lord will find new strength. They will soar high on wings like eagles. They will run and not grow weary. They will walk and not faint." Isaiah 40:31 NLT

WHAT DO A CEILING fan, a fluorescent light, a tapping pencil, an itchy sweater, a piece of chewing gum, and a crooked picture on the wall have in common? For most of your students, probably nothing, other than the fact that they may be items in their Sunday school classroom. However, if you have a student with autism, ADHD, or another special need, even one of these things can mean the difference between a good day and a bad day in your classroom or small group. And just when you think you have adequately addressed one of the issues, another one that you absolutely did not expect may arise.

It is very likely that any of the groups that you work with at church may include at least a few students with special needs. Often, students with Autism Spectrum Disorders and ADHD may have some of the most difficult behaviors to manage in a group setting. While there are some excellent full-length books available that contain many more specific details, the goal of this chapter is to provide you with a basic overview and some practical ideas that can be immediately implemented in your work with kids in a church setting.

Autism

Depending on when you started working with children, you may be familiar with related diagnostic terms like Autistic Disorder, Rett Syndrome, Asperger Syndrome, or Pervasive Developmental Disorder: Not Otherwise Specified (PDD-NOS). With the latest version of the *Diagnostic and Statistical Manual of Mental Disorders,* the *DSM-V-TR,* published by the American Psychiatric Association in 2022, all of these terms have now been combined into one label: Autism Spectrum Disorder (ASD).[1]

There is a common saying which goes something like this—"If you know one child with autism, you know one child with autism." Because ASD is indeed a spectrum, every child comes with their own wiring and falls at a different place on the spectrum. While it is helpful to understand the dynamics of autism so you can better work with your students, there are no cookie cutter autistic students, so needs and behaviors can be very different from one student to another.

In a nutshell, to be diagnosed with ASD, a person must meet all three of these criteria:

1. Difficulties with social-emotional reciprocity—struggles with social interactions including two-way conversations, sharing interests, and expressing or understanding emotions
2. Difficulties in non-verbal communications—struggles with social interactions including eye contact, body language, facial expressions, and/or gestures
3. Difficulties in developing and maintaining relationships (other than with caregivers)—this can include a lack of interest in others, struggles in responding to different social contexts, and difficulty sharing imaginative play with others.

---

1. American Psychiatric Association, *DSM-V-TR.* 299.00.

Additionally, in diagnosing, individuals must demonstrate at least two of these four behaviors:

1. Stereotyped speech, repetitive motor movement, repetitive use of objects or abnormal phrases, and repeating words or phrases (sometimes from TV shows, songs, or other people)
2. Ritualized patterns of behaviors (verbal or non-verbal), rigid adherence to routines and extreme resistance to change
3. Restricted interests with abnormal focus, such as strong attachment to unusual objects (i.e. patterns, rocks, numbers) or obsessions with certain interests (i.e. historical events, airplanes, insects, taking things apart). Note: Just because you have an interest or a hobby, this does not place you on the spectrum! It is only when it is at an obsessive level and is combined with other characteristics.
4. Reactivity (increased or decreased) to sensory input like disliking sounds, excessive touching or smelling, fascination with spinning objects, or not reacting to pain. (I have worked with many students who would wear the same coat all day long every day, even in 100-degree weather!)

There are also three severity levels within the ASD diagnosis to help describe the level of need for each individual–

1. Level 1—Requiring Support: Difficulty initiating social interactions, unusual responses to social advances, decreased interest in social interactions; repetitive behaviors may interfere with daily functioning. There may be some difficulty in redirecting from fixed interests.
2. Level 2—Requiring Substantial Support: Marked delays in verbal and non-verbal communication, difficulty forming social relationships, restricted interests and repetitive behaviors. There may be high levels of distress when interests or behaviors are interrupted.
3. Level 3—Requiring Very Substantial Support: Severe impairment in daily functioning and very limited initiation of social

interaction or verbal communication abilities. Fixed rituals and repetitive behaviors greatly interfere with functioning. It is very difficult to redirect the individual from interests or help them cope with change.

Now that you know a little more about the ASD diagnosis itself, let's think about what this means in a ministry setting. Students on the spectrum may have difficulty understanding abstract concepts, using spontaneous communication for social interactions (especially with other children), and engaging in imaginary thinking. However, while the diagnosis gives us an answer to some of the behaviors we may see, it also provides an opportunity to find ways to prepare the student to be successful when faced with new experiences. Some of the most recent evidence-based interventions recommended by the National Autism Center include schedules, social stories, and modeling.[2]

Schedules

Visual schedules help make new experiences more predictable. Having a schedule of activities posted each time a student enters children's church or a Wednesday night youth activity provides a preview of activities and transitions ahead of time. This helps the student prepare for what is coming and takes the fear out of what is coming next. As the session begins, review the schedule with students and point to and name the items on the list. As you transition to each new activity, remind students where you are at in the agenda. If you are not able to keep the schedule up for the entire session, suggest students take a picture so they can reference it or bring back up the schedule on a slide at transition points.

Some sessions with your students will more naturally contain more disorder, like a trunk-or-treat harvest party in the parking lot, or a Christmas party where students may be running all over the church on a scavenger hunt. The more chaotic the activity or lesson,

---

2. National Autism Center, *Findings and Conclusions: National Standards Project, Phase 2*.

the more you will need to prepare your ASD student for what is coming. Consider emailing the schedule to the parents of the student ahead of time so that they can review it together in advance. Or hold a brief meeting after church the week before the event so you can talk with the student and parent about what they can expect and how to plan. This will require some advanced planning on your part, but it will pay off tremendously in the ways that the student is able to successfully engage in your activity.

Social Stories

Social stories help students understand what to expect in specific situations. Remember that change can be frightening for ASD students (and many others as well), so you empower your students when you help them to understand the change that is coming. For example, consider this social story about communion:

> *Tanner, Caroline, and Alisa all go to different churches. Each one of their churches participates in the sacrament of communion, but each church does it a little differently.*
>
> *In Tanner's church, when it is time for communion, the ushers dismiss the people by rows and they all go up to the front to take communion. The pastor or elder holds out the bread and each person takes one piece. Then the person dips the bread into the juice and eats it right there in front before going back to their seat.* (This can even be acted out depending on the student's level of need and understanding.)
>
> *In Caroline's church, they do a lot of things like Tanner's church does. Everyone lines up and goes to the front to take communion, but the pastor or elder takes the bread and dips it in the juice and then gives it to the person at the top of their fingers. The person then places it in their mouth themselves. Then they go back and sit down.*

Check for Understanding: What is the same about Tanner and Caroline's churches in how they take communion? What is different?

At Alisa's church they pass out the communion elements differently. Everyone stays in their seats and the pastors and elders pass the communion plates down each row. Those plates look like this (holds one up or draws a picture). When the plate goes by each person, you take one piece of bread and one cup of juice and then hand the plate to the person sitting beside you. The plates can be heavy, so you have to be careful. At Alisa's church, instead of everyone taking communion at a different time, everyone must wait until the communion elements have been handed out to everyone. Then, once everyone has some, the entire congregation takes it together at one time.

This is why I am telling you this story. There may be a time when you go to a different church and they take communion differently. This is okay! How do we typically take communion at our church? (Student(s) answer.) *Yes, like at Tanner's church. However, on Christmas Eve this year, we are going to do something different. There will be a lot of candles and decorations in the front of the sanctuary and there will not be enough room for people to stand in a line for communion like we usually do. So instead, we are going to take communion like they do at Alisa's church. Do you remember what that looks like? Tell me about it.* (Pause for responses.) *Good! Do you think we can take communion that way this time?* (Give student(s) processing time.) *Excellent. Let's practice passing a communion plate that I have so we can know what to expect.*

In this short social story, can you see how preparing a student or group of students for something new will be helpful for them? While social stories are tremendously helpful for your students with ASD, they are not restrictive to this group alone. Oftentimes *all* of your students can benefit from reading, hearing, or participating in a social story.

Modeling and Language Training

Modeling means showing a child or teen how to do what is expected. Practicing passing the communion plate in the last example was modeling. The goal is to show them from start to finish what something is supposed to look or sound like, from beginning to end, and then give them plenty of time to practice. Sometimes modeling involves not only an action, but also the wording or terminology that may go with it.

Our church recently changed what had been called "greeting time" into "passing the peace." Instead of just shaking a hand and saying hello at a specific point in the service, our charge was to actually verbalize the sharing of Christ's peace with each other. As you grasp someone's hand, one person states, "The peace of the Lord be with you," and the other person replies, "And also with you." I love that our children's pastor also implemented this in children's church!

The first time that it was introduced, she shared why it was important and had students practice what to say. (Remember the Direct Instruction Model from Chapter 2—"I do, we do, you do"? It works perfectly here.) First, she models for them what it looks like by being two different characters. (Putting on a hat works great here to be a different person.) That models the "I do." Then, she called up a volunteer to wear the hat and be the other person to practice what to say. ("We do.") Finally, she had all of the children practice with each other what to say and do when it was time to pass the peace. ("You do.")

As you can see, modeling does not always have to take a lot of time. This example took less than three minutes. This can also be done on an individual or whole group level. Make sure that you always follow with praise and compliments on what you saw working really well.

Also, remember that practice and review may be necessary throughout the year. A student may have been absent the first time it was modeled, or they may simply forget if it is not part of a regular routine. It is not a bad thing to revisit an expectation or procedure when needed—that is great teaching! Classroom teachers typically have to revisit expectations, procedures, or routines after Christmas and spring break because the students have been gone for a while and are out of practice. Whenever there has been a gap in getting together with your group, plan a few minutes of reminders and practice as needed.

Other Helpful Tips

Avoid Sensory Overload—A student with ASD who walks into a youth room with flashing lights, blaring music, loud voices, and new smells coming from the snack table will most likely freak out or completely isolate. Every part of their senses will be on overload and they will be unable to handle it all at once. Whenever you are planning an event or activity which involves a sensory change (vision, hearing, touch, smell, or kinesthetic response), it is best to only introduce one new change at a time, as opposed to many at once. However, if there is a time when you know sensory stimuli will be turned up, talk to the student and parent ahead of time so they are prepared for what they will experience and can choose what will best help them cope. This could be something as simple as noise canceling earphones, sun glasses, or arriving to the scene early so they can see each sensory item as it is integrated into the setting. You could also have them help you set up the room and turn on the light board or music so you can gauge what levels they are comfortable with. Planning ahead like this helps build trust between you and the student and minimizes surprises.

Keep Language Concrete—Autistic students rarely understand idioms the first time they hear them (i.e. a fork in the road; break a leg; it's a piece of cake; on the fence, etc.). Their brains tend to understand things very literally and they are not able to correctly decipher the meaning of the idiomatic expression by defining or visualizing the individual words. Try to avoid using idioms, or if there is a specific reason to use them, make sure to teach their meaning and provide visuals to demonstrate what you mean. If you need a better understanding of what an ASD student might be thinking, read some children's stories written by Peggy and Herman Parrish about housekeeper Amelia Bedelia, who takes all of her employer's instructions literally. It will help you better understand your students and how you can change your use of language to help them be more successful.

Avoid Sarcasm—Because students with ASD have difficulty with social interactions and understanding emotions, they can have a very hard time understanding sarcasm and may take sarcastic speech literally. This can be extremely frustrating because they do not understand when people are joking or teasing, and it may further increase their isolation from others.

Be Predictable—Your ASD students will take comfort in knowing what they can expect from you from week to week, so even minor changes, like wearing a funny wig or changing the seating arrangement, can be very disturbing to them. Whenever you anticipate making a change, just give the family a quick phone call or send an email so that they can help prepare their student. If you call the student and let them know that you will look a little different on Wednesday night, then it becomes a game to see how quickly they can figure out what is new.

Directly Teach Social Skills—Do not ever assume that your students will know how to appropriately respond to a situation. There may be some sort of cognitive disability present, but they also just might not have ever been exposed to something like that before. For example, students new to church may not know that in some places, wearing a baseball cap in the sanctuary might be considered offensive. Talking with them about why your church considers this important will be helpful and will protect them from potential glares from older people in the church. In the same way, though, if an autistic student needs a comfort item like a hat or headphones, then it is also helpful for you to help the rest of the students or congregation understand why the student will be using those things in church until they get comfortable enough to remove them.

Use Visuals (pictures and modeling)—Visuals are a powerful tool for learning for all students, regardless of age, but they are especially helpful for your struggling learners, multi-language learners, and students with ASD. A simple picture from Google

Images or a projected map may make the difference between understanding and confusion.

Treat Students as Individuals—Remember that no two autistic students are the same. Each has unique needs and life experiences that have helped shape them. Just because something worked for one ASD student in your youth group last year, it does not necessarily mean that it will work for a new student this year. Getting to know your students will help you better understand how you can best care for them and point them toward the God who made them and knows everything about them.

ADHD

Attention Deficit Hyperactivity Disorder (ADHD) is not a new phenomenon. The earliest documented mention of its symptoms was from Hippocrates, who is traditionally referred to as the father of medicine and lived in Greece from about 460 to 375 BC. He believed the cause was an "overbalance of fire over water" and recommended a bland diet (fish, but not a lot of other meat), lots of water, and plenty of physical exercise. A Scottish physician, Sir Andrew Crichton, described a "disease of attention" in his book published in 1798 and observed that people with this condition seemed to have a hard time sticking with a task for long periods of time. Medical textbooks in the 1800s used terms like "nervous child," "mental instability," and "simple hyperexcitability."

In 1968, the *DSM-II* included the disorder, but used the term "hyperkinetic reaction of childhood." The next revision, the *DSM-III*, in 1980, named it Attention Deficit Disorder (ADD), with or without hyperactivity. In 1987, the American Psychiatric Association changed the name from ADD to ADHD.[3] Today, the *DSM-V-TR* lists three different presentations of the disorder which can present themselves differently throughout a person's lifetime: inattentive type, hyperactive/impulsive type, and combined type.[4]

3. CHADD, "More Fire than Water: A Short History of ADHD," 2.
4. American Psychiatric Association, *DSM-V-TR*. 299.00.

While it is very normal for children to occasionally have difficulties concentrating and behaving, those diagnosed with ADHD will not simply grow out of these behaviors. They may talk too much, fidget, daydream, forget or lose things, make careless mistakes, act impulsively, struggle with taking turns, and have difficulty getting along with others. The symptoms can often be so severe that if left untreated, they have lasting negative effects at home, school, and with peers.[5] I have found that there often tends to be more empathy from adults directed towards autistic students than students with ADHD. It is almost as if as a society we incorrectly see ADHD less as a disorder and more as a temporary state that the student needs to work harder to overcome. This can lead to tremendous frustration for both the church worker and the student.

The *DSM-V* describes the three ways that ADHD can present itself, and these can change over time for an individual. The severity of symptoms can be designated as mild, moderate, or severe.

Predominantly Inattentive Presentation—Individuals can be easily distracted and can forget daily routines. They struggle to organize or complete a task. Following instructions or conversations can be difficult.

Predominantly Hyperactive-Impulsive Presentation—Individuals have a hard time sitting still and fidget and/or talk excessively. There is a great feeling of restlessness and it is difficult for them to control impulses. This makes it difficult for them to wait their turn or follow directions, and so impulsivity may lead to interrupting, grabbing objects away from others, or blurting out at the wrong time. Younger children may run, jump, or climb at inappropriate times. Accidents and injuries can often be the result of their impulsiveness.

Combined Presentation—Symptoms of the two times are equally present.

As though these challenges alone are not enough, more than half of the students with ADHD also have learning disabilities, and

---

5. Faraone, "208 Evidence-Based Conclusions About the Disorder," 789-818.

many also exhibit some sort of emotional or behavioral disorder. Statistically, adolescents with ADHD are more likely to prematurely experiment with alcohol, tobacco, and drugs.[6]

ADHD Tips

How can we, as the church, help our students with ADHD be more successful and feel like a church or youth group is a safe place where they belong?

- Consistency is important. Keep routines.
- Keep supplies and procedures organized (coats, papers, markers, etc.).
- Plan ahead for transitions and complex tasks.
- Reward positive behaviors.
- Use a high degree of structure in every lesson.
- Provide breaks.
- Seat the student next to positive role models and close to the front of the room or a place where there are fewer distractions.
- Include physical activity as often as possible.
- Break long projects or games into smaller parts.
- Make sure all assignments or tasks are clear and provide both in writing and aloud. Remember that they may not be able to hold a lot of information in their minds for very long.
- Ask students to repeat back directions to check for understanding.
- Use a timer or sound signal to help with time management.

---

6. CHADD, "About ADHD—Overview," 1-3.

- Provide tools to help with organization: folders, cubbies, seat assignments, etc.
- Limit overly repetitive assignments or tasks that are too difficult. Fidgeting can often be either a symptom of boredom or overstimulation.
- Provide highlighters, graphic organizers, summaries, or word lists whenever there is a lot to read.

There are also many things that you can do to create a positive environment and support appropriate behavior.

- Use a talking stick or another object which can be passed around and indicates whose turn it is to speak.
- Develop a private signal to help a student recognize when their behavior is escalating. (Think of behavioral prompts as a reminder instead of a reprimand.)
- Promote self-awareness—Ask the student to describe the problem or issue. Ask them why they think it is happening and how they can change their behavior. If the student needs some quiet time away, ask them to draw a picture or use words to describe their feelings, actions, and improvement plan.
- Support the student's participation in small groups.
- Encourage students to see things from multiple points of view. Students with ADHD will not normally be able to do this on their own.
- Find opportunities for their peers to see them in a positive light so the student feels connected and welcomed in the group.

Students with ADHD can seem to live in a world of extremes and be "managed by the moment." Their focus, behavior, and interests can change very quickly. But, with the challenges also come enormous energy and drive. Their spontaneity, creativity, and fast thinking can help them to be fun to be around and very successful. Sports figures like Michael Phelps, Simone Biles, and Michael Jordan all have ADHD. While not officially diagnosed, some of the characteristics displayed by famous historical figures like Albert Einstein, Wolfgang Amadeus Mozart, Thomas Edison, and Sir Isaac Newton lead us to believe that they may have had ADHD tendencies.

Even though the word "deficit" is in the title, never think about ADHD as a disorder in the typical sense. The label simply gives us indication that we are working with a student who may think, learn, and behave differently. Dr. William Sears wrote in 1998, "AD[H]D left unrecognized and not carefully managed can become a disability. If understood, accepted, valued, and shaped, these traits can work to the child's advantage."[7]

Support for Parents

Parents with special needs students can often feel embarrassed and alienated. They feel as if they are being judged by others because of their child's behavior. Many parents feel like they are blamed by society—as if autism, ADHD, or another disability was their fault. When a meltdown happens in public, like at a grocery store or shopping center, the parent quickly becomes the focus of critical stares of disbelief, loud sighs, and shaking heads by strangers who are quick to ridicule. The truth is, parents of special needs students deserve medals, not condemnation! The last thing we want to happen is for families to stop attending church because they do not feel like there is a place for them or their child where they can each be loved and encouraged.

As you are working to find ways to help a student with special needs be successful in your Sunday school classroom or youth group, remember to include the parent in the conversation. Partnering with parents and guardians is one of the most powerful ways to ensure the success of the student. In the process, remember that as you work to build trust with the primary caregiver as

---

7. Sears, *The ADD Book: New Understandings, New Approaches to Parenting Your Child*, 37.

an ally, that parent or grandparent may also have their own needs that your church can help address. While a simple hug or an empathetic listening ear is important, the parents of the special needs students at your church may benefit from a support group or specific connection with others in the congregation who currently have or have had some of the same challenges.

As you begin to apply some of the concepts in this chapter, you may have moments where you feel some guilt about ways in the past that you responded to a student with special needs in trying to punish a behavior that the student could not control. Remind yourself that you did the best that you could with what you knew at that time and concentrate on the positive ways that you can move forward in the present and beyond with these new ideas.

One of my most important tips in working with special needs students for more than three decades is remembering to pray for patience, wisdom, and specifically for that child by name. God knows everything about them, and God can show you how to love them the way that he does. Go early to the classroom or your youth room and sit in the chair where that student will sit. Pray that you will have renewed energy and that they will have open eyes, ears, and a heart to hear the message that they need that day. Look for a way that you can make a new connection. God has placed you in the life of this child for a reason. You can trust God and rely on God's strength and empowerment for what this day holds.

Chapter 5 Reflection Questions

1. What are some of the key characteristics of students on the autism spectrum? What about ADHD?
2. Why is it important to treat each child as an individual, regardless of their diagnosis?
3. Think about your classroom or group space. What changes to the environment might be helpful for ASD or ADHD students?

4. What are some of the biggest joys of working with students with these developmental conditions?

5. How might your church better support the parents of students with special needs?

6

Language and Culture

"So now you are no longer strangers and aliens. Rather, you are fellow citizens with God's people, and you belong to God's household. As God's household, you are built on the foundation of the apostles and prophets with Christ Jesus himself as the cornerstone." Ephesians 2:19-22 CEB

AMONG THE BEAUTIFUL DIVERSITY that is the body of Christ, language and culture differences may exist that can either serve to separate us from each other or unify us together as God's people.

Our children were in elementary school when we moved overseas to work at a Christian international school in South Korea. Some of the first terms we had to consciously remove from our vocabulary were "weird," "odd," "strange," "gross," and "crazy" when referencing foods and customs that were new to us. Instead, we practiced over and over, "that is *different* from what I am used to." Whether you identify it easily or not, much of who you are is tied together within the complex strands of your language and culture. As you work with children and teens who may have a different language or cultural base than your own, understanding that they may hear and see the world differently than you is one of the first steps in building a positive and lasting relationship with them.

Multilingual Learners

It is estimated that by 2025, one out of every four students in public schools in the United States will be second-language learners whose native language is not English. They are the fastest growing demographic of students in k-12 classrooms.[1] The acronyms have changed over time, but these are some helpful terms to know: EL (English learner), ELL (English language learner), ENL (English as a new language), ESL (English as a second language) and ML (Multilingual learner) or MLL (Multilingual language learner). As a profession, education is moving toward using the preferred term "ML" because students tend to be continuously developing proficiencies in multiple languages at the same time (usually their native language and then English). Focusing on just the "English Learner" aspect fails to recognize that they may already be fluent or proficient in another language and their knowledge of that language may continue to develop while they are also learning English.

MLs may look very different from each other. Consider these examples:

Emilia had a strong academic background before coming to the United States as an exchange student. She is literate in her native language of German and started studying English in her local public school in Frankfurt when she was eight years old. Emilia is staying with a host family who attend your church and will be with them for one school year.

Aadan is originally from Sudan and has very limited formal schooling due to war in his native country. He has limited literacy skills in his native language and has significant gaps in his educational background. He also has had limited exposure to school

---

1. National Education Association, *English Language Learners*.

routines and expectations. His family is currently divided and he has not seen his father in five years.

Chun was born in the United States and speaks both Mandarin and English with her parents and siblings at home. While she can fluently speak both languages, her reading and writing is not yet proficient in both languages. Chun loves to play the piano and practices every day.

Manuel was born in the United States but only speaks Spanish with his grandmother and siblings at home. He started learning English in kindergarten, but has attended five different elementary schools in three different states. Due to his family's migrant status, they move geographically based on the harvest seasons. His conversational English skills are strong, but he lacks academic vocabulary skills in both Spanish and English. He is embarrassed to read out loud in front of his peers in either language.

Now that you have met each of these students, consider what unique needs they may have if they were to start attending your children's program or youth group. How can you help them not only feel welcome in your church, but also make sure that the messages you are trying to convey are heard and understood?

If you grew up in a culture in which your native language was the dominant or majority language spoken, you may not yet have a lot of context for what it feels like to be an "outsider" linguistically. One of the first assignments I give my students in my Teaching MLs course is to intentionally put themselves in a situation where they do not speak or understand the language being spoken around them. This can be done by attending a local church service delivered in a different language or even watching a classroom lesson online presented in a language they do not know. After this experience, I typically hear comments like this . . .

"I lost interest after the first few minutes. Even though I was trying to concentrate, I just could not."

"I kept falling asleep!"

"I started doing things like fidgeting, staring at my watch, or looking around the room or out the window."

"I felt so lost and stupid!"

If the procedures also included things like standing and sitting at certain times, reciting a pledge or verse, or being called on to respond, their anxiety and confusion grew even faster to the point that they wanted to quit long before the session was over.

However, when I ask what helped them pay attention, these are some of the responses I typically receive . . .

"The teacher used his hands a lot to motion what he meant or what we should do next."

"We sang a song in their language that I knew in English, and so it helped me follow along with the meaning more easily."

"She put up pictures or wrote down key words and that helped me better understand."

"The people around me smiled and nodded and really seemed like they wanted to help me."

Even though this assignment only has to last about an hour, the experience is a powerful one. Most importantly, it helps them grow in their empathy and increases their desire to help instruction be more deliberate and meaningful to their students who are not native English speakers. I would encourage you this week to find a way to put yourself in the shoes of a second-language learner and think about how you might adjust your lessons to make them more accessible for multilingual learners.

Language Stages

Even after a student has been in an English-speaking country or classroom for a few years, they still may not be fluent or proficient in English. It is important to understand the progression that a person (young or old) usually goes through to learn a new language.

1. In the silent/receptive phase, the learner primarily listens and tries to pick up specific functional vocabulary. Survival language is typically the focus of speech. Terms like hello, please, thank you, more, no, yes, some food names, and questions like "where is the bathroom?" tend to come first.

LANGUAGE AND CULTURE

2. As the learner progresses in the language, he or she has the confidence to start speaking more often. Pronunciation is more rudimentary (and may sound a bit like baby talk), but words and basic phrases are used more often by the learner than in the previous stage. Patience and empathy from adults and peers are really important at this stage so they do not feel embarrassed or isolate themselves.

3. Eventually, with a lot of practice, the learner continues to add new words and can start speaking in longer phrases and ultimately, full sentences, including the ability and confidence to ask questions in the new language. If they have more formal education in the language, reading and writing begins to develop here too.

4. Once the learner has at least 6,000 words in their new language vocabulary, their pronunciation tends to improve and they feel more comfortable talking with people, especially if they have a conversation partner or a way to daily practice hearing, reading, and speaking the language.[2]

The timeline to learn a new language varies greatly based on the motivation of the student and the access to quality instruction. But every study on language acquisition confirms the same thing—Learning a language takes years, not months! It is *not* a quick or easy process. Additionally, parents who are new to a country have even less time to study due to working, so often they rely on their children to translate for them or relay important information.

Remember that it is easier to learn survival/conversational vocabulary first, because that is what we use most often. Academic and subject-specific vocabulary usually needs to be explicitly taught. Even native English speakers may encounter terminology in the Bible that is new to them. Flip through your Bible and look at a passage through the lens of an English language learner or someone new to faith. Torah, advent, covenant, sanctification, Messiah, sacrament, apostle . . . are just a few of the thousands of

---

2. IRIS, "Second Language Acquisition," 1.

specific biblical terms that need to be taught in context as students are studying specific passages.

It is also helpful to remind students that sometimes we use the same words differently. "Grace" and "Faith" are important biblical principles, but they can also be girls' names. "Lost" and "Born Again " are two examples of commonly terms used in the church, but students need to understand when terms like these are intended to be figurative or literal. The Old Testament contains many unfamiliar names of people, tribes, and locations. It's okay for students to know that even native English speakers stumble over those words sometimes!

As you look back over the language learning progression, remember that students will often understand more auditorily at first than what they can speak back to you. You also need to provide processing time because they often have to translate the word or question into their native language first, derive an answer, and then translate it back into English. This takes time!

Caution: Do not assume that a head nod means that someone understands. During my time as a school counselor in South Korea, it was a moment of epiphany when I realized just how much I nodded my head when a parent was talking to me in Hangul, even though I had no idea what they were saying! As you are working with MLs, it is important to check for understanding often to make sure that they are really comprehending your intent. The following story helps to emphasize why this is important.

Idioms

As you read in the last chapter, idiomatic language can be very stressful for students with special needs who take words literally. Why in the world would that person tell me to "break a leg" before going on stage? How can it possibly be "raining cats and dogs" outside? In the same way, second-language learners are another group that can become quickly confused when you use a term that may have a double meaning that they do not understand.

LANGUAGE AND CULTURE

One of my favorite stories to emphasize this point came from a college student who was taking one of my classes which focuses on working with multilingual learners. When we started discussing the danger of idioms and other monikers, she shared this example with us ... The year before, their family had hosted an exchange student from Western Europe at their home. His English was very strong, but that did not necessarily mean that he understood all of the local dialect and references. In church one Sunday, shortly after he arrived in the United States, the pastor mentioned something about walking barefoot in a field of *goat heads*. If you are from a hot and dry climate, you understand the reference was to the little puncture vines which can flatten your bike tire, get stuck in your tennis shoes, or really hurt if you step on one barefooted. The family had not thought anything about it until they got in the car after the service and realized that their exchange student was really traumatized by the reference. "Where is the field with all of the bloody heads from dead goats, and why would that pastor walk through it without shoes?" he cried out. That one reference was completely appalling to him and he was not able to concentrate on anything else during the sermon because all he could picture was a field which contained the heads of thousands of dead goats, and he wanted to stay as far away from that place as he could.

His host sister quickly pulled up a picture of a puncture vine on her phone and showed him how the burrs can resemble the head of a goat when they are broken off from the vine. In less than 30 seconds, his fears were subdued, and he now knew what types of vines to avoid when bike riding. However, he had missed the message of the sermon because of one very minor reference that he did not understand. As you are working with multilingual learners or even just students from a different geographic location than your own, try to avoid jargon or idioms. If it is necessary to use specific terminology that might be confusing, make sure you pause for a minute to show a picture or clearly describe what you mean and then check for understanding before moving on to make sure your students really understand what you were talking about.

Helpful Tips

- Speak slowly. (But not loudly. They can usually hear you just fine!)
- Use pictures, visuals, and manipulatives.
- Turn on closed captioning for videos when it is available.
- Allow ML students to use their phones as needed for translation help.
- Use hand gestures when it helps solidify meaning (and is not culturally offensive).
- Project or write out new key vocabulary. Pronounce it a few times together if it is a term you want them to remember and say correctly.
- Provide the Bible passage or lesson concepts to students ahead of time.
- Provide extra processing time before you ask for an answer.
- Have the ML student sit next to another student who will be a reassuring conversation partner.
- Create an environment where all students are encouraged to learn and grow together.
- Be caring and supportive!

If you are interested in learning a new language, perhaps to acquire some basic vocabulary in the native language of one of your students, Duolingo, Babbel, and Rosetta Stone are excellent language apps you can put on your phone or device to help you begin your journey.

I love walking into church rooms where the native language of all of the students is somehow on display. For example, you could have a poster with the ways to say "God" or "Amen" in different languages. This serves as not only a welcoming place for speakers of other languages, but it also helps native English speakers remember that people all around the world worship God in different languages.

Refugees

Depending on where you live, some of the MLs that you work with may be refugees. As defined by the U.S. *Immigration and Nationality Act,* a refugee is a person who has left their country of nationality and is "unable or unwilling to return to that country due to persecution or a well-founded fear of persecution based upon race, religion, nationality, membership in a specific social group, or political group."[3]

Most refugees have a first language other than English. However, it is important to note that they also have a lot of other circumstances that make them different from what we might consider more traditional second-language learners. Children and adults with refugee status may have encountered exposure to violence and trauma which can impact cognitive, emotional and behavioral development. Children may have had disruptions to their schooling or no access to schooling at all.

The parents of refugee students have their own set of challenges as they are trying to hold their families together while everyone adapts to a new environment. It is likely the parents are also struggling with unfamiliar cultural values and behavioral patterns that they see their children adopting, many of which may have been considered disrespectful in the culture of their original locality.

While many of the things discussed in the upcoming trauma chapter may apply to refugees, here are some additional considerations from the International Rescue Committee[4] for your children's program or youth group:

---

3. Immigration and Nationality Act, 2004.

4. International Rescue Committee, *Refugee Children and Youth Backgrounders,* 1-28.

- Refugee students may not have internet access at home or transportation to events.
- Trust and safety are not necessarily their assumptions. They may not initially believe that adults or other students will not hurt them.
- Some students may not be accustomed to adults talking to them individually or asking them to express their opinions.
- It is possible that the family has been separated (temporarily or permanently) and/or living with someone that they do not know well.
- Refugee students may not necessarily know what to do with crayons, scissors, sports equipment, permission slips, etc.
- Refugees may be uncomfortable in American clothing and unfamiliar with American hygiene practices. They may not have steady access to laundry facilities.
- Restrooms with separate stalls and flushing toilets may be new to them.
- Refugees may not understand that when they get on a bus or van, it will bring them back to the church afterwards.

Here are some additional ways you can assist your students and their families . . .

- Handouts, flyers, and projected text should be typed because they can be more easily translated by software apps.
- Parents may be uncomfortable or intimidated by your church's programming for kids. Invite parents or family members to attend alongside their child whenever they would like to.

- Offer an orientation session or record a video with captions that parents and students can reference with the activities and resources your church has available.
- Provide group transportation when possible.
- In situations where students are not allowed to use cell phones, allow your refugee and ML students to use their phones if they are needed for translation.
- Research the cultural norms of the country where the student is from. Note that sometimes eye contact, body language, and hand signals can mean different things than what you may be used to.
- Provide food and childcare at meetings with parents to encourage higher participation.

It may also be very meaningful for your refugee students to talk about Jesus as a refugee. Yes, he had to leave heaven to come to earth as a human, but students may more closely connect with the fact that Jesus and his parents had to escape to Egypt because they were fleeing persecution from Herod, who was trying to kill them. Some of Jesus's earliest years were spent living the life of a refugee. Truly, he knows what they are experiencing.

Third-Culture Kids

Sociologist Ruth Useem coined the term "third-culture kid" in the 1950s to identify the unique characteristics and needs of expatriate children who spend the majority of their formative years overseas. Someone's first culture refers to the culture of their parents. The second culture is that of the country or countries in which the child has lived, if they are different from their first culture. Therefore, the "third culture" is the fusion of both the culture of the child's parents and the culture in which the child was raised. TCKs often adopt certain traits of each culture to create their own unique cultural identity. Today, this might be a student in your youth group whose parents have worked overseas for an extended length of time in the military or a global business, or a missionary kid whose family has returned to the United States after serving internationally. Sometimes students who have grown up as immigrants, refugees, International adoptees, or the children of minority or bi-cultural parents may also resonate with some of the characteristics of TCKs.

TCKs often feel like they live between worlds. They have relationships with each of the cultures, but do not have full ownership of any one culture. No one question gets at the heart of their struggle more than when they are asked, "Where are you from?" The pause and hesitancy to answer will be because they do not know how they should answer or if you really want to know the details. Often TCKs will use the term "passport country" to identify their citizenship, but it does not necessarily mean that they have any strong connections with that country of origin or can talk about any of the local customs or tourist attractions. If a Caucasian student answers, "Venezuela," or "China," they can be met with stares and even the perplexed follow-up statement, "Well, you do not look Asian." (Believe me, they *love* that one!)

The population of TCKs and CCKs (cross-cultural kids) continues to grow and receive more attention in our globalized society. Former President Barack Obama is a third-culture kid who was born to an American mother and a Kenyan father. He spent many of his formative years in Indonesia and Hawaii. "I was raised as an Indonesian child and a Hawaiian child and as a black child and as a white child," Obama later recalled. "And so, what I benefited from is a multiplicity of cultures that all fed me."[5]

TCKs can develop a great sense of inner confidence and self-reliance. They may not always like change, but they expect it and learn to cope with new situations. They tend to have keen linguistic and observation skills developed from years of having to navigate between cultures. This learning has sometimes come at a great price because of the lack of time to grieve and process when things around them change quickly. Younger TCKs wonder if it is worth making friendships again if they know they might be

---

5. Nelson, *Barack Obama: Life Before the Presidency*. 1.

moving soon. On the flip side, older TCKs often form strong and lasting bonds with others who have had TCK experiences because they share common experiences—even if the countries and purposes for being there were completely different.

One of my favorite resources on this topic is David Pollock and Ruth Van Reken's *Third-Culture Kids: Growing Up Among Worlds*, an international bestseller now in its third edition.[6] It contains stories and research specifically on TCKs and the blessings and challenges of students who have grown up multiculturally. In addition to a wealth of examples and insights, they include a chapter specifically on reentry and what adults can do to help make the transition smoother and continue to care for students who may be returning home to a place that they have never really known. The latest edition also contains a "stages and needs" tool that is designed to help families and organizations identify and meet the needs of TCKs.

The Bible is filled with examples of third-culture kids and adults: Abraham, Joseph, Moses, Daniel, Esther, and Jesus Christ, just to name a few. As you learn more about TCKs and go back and read through their stories in the Bible, it will shed a whole new light on their struggles and the ways in which they interpreted and interacted with the world around them. Talking about the experiences of these biblical figures with your TCKs is empowering because it helps them grasp the ways God can use them and their unique experiences in the kingdom.

Cultural Incidents

Craig Storti, in his book *The Art of Crossing Cultures*, asserts ". . . because of cultural differences—different, deeply held beliefs and instincts about what is natural, normal, right, and good—cross-cultural interactions are subject to all manner of confusion, misunderstanding, and interpretation."[7] The outcome that no one

---

6. Van Reken, *Third Culture Kids 3rd Edition: Growing Up Among Worlds.*
7. Storti, *The Art of Crossing Cultures*, 25.

desires is to have diminished effectiveness because of a culture misstep. But how can you identify when culture is a factor in the communication or miscommunication?

One of the first steps in successful interaction with people of other cultures is to first acknowledge our own cultural conditioning and our ethnocentric tendency to expect that other people are like us. We expect, and even depend, on certain responses because those responses are part of our cultural norms. This is the source of most cross-cultural incidents. The person from Culture A was expecting the person from Culture B to speak, respond, or react like the people from Culture A. When the person from Culture B instead responds like someone from Culture B, it can create an incident that can create confusion, hurt feelings, or even be severely offensive, while the person from Culture B has no idea what has just transpired. It is our *expectation* of their behavior, not their behavior itself, that is at the true heart of the matter.

While there are many different examples of the ways that this plays out, how different cultures address the issue of time is one that you may have already noticed. In the summer of 2024, our family traveled to Kenya to conduct some workshops for local secondary teachers in Nairobi. We had prepared a full day's worth of material and had arrived early to make sure everything was ready. The clock struck 8:00 a.m. and we were ready to begin, but the conference room held only about 15 of the 100 teachers who had registered. "Oh, don't worry," our host reassured us. "They are just on Kenyan time." Sure enough, more began to slowly trickle in and by about 10:00 a.m., the room was full and the teachers were eager to participate and learn some new teaching strategies. Even though I knew that different cultures define punctuality differently, I was still surprised by my own emotions. We had traveled a long way and had limited time to cover a lot of material. As much as I was trying not to be offended, I could feel my frustration rise as the morning dragged on and there were still empty seats.

At about 9:30, I had to remind myself of an "ah-ha" moment I had the first time I read Storti's book. The process of becoming more culturally effective looks something like this:

1. We expect other people to behave like we do, but they do not.
2. A cultural incident occurs.
3. We react (with anger, frustration, hurt, etc.).
4. We become aware of our own reactions . . .
5. . . . and realized it is our own behavior that has contributed to the cultural incident (expecting cultural sameness).
6. We are more motivated to learn about Culture B, and start to expect them to behave like themselves.
7. There are less cultural incidents.[8]

This may seem like a simple example, and if you always start youth group two hours late, it will be over before it really begins! But as you begin thinking about issues you are having with students and their parents, it is wise to consider if it may potentially be a cultural issue that deserves some further investigation. As you learn more about your students and their backgrounds, either through research or simply asking them questions, when appropriate, it will become easier to navigate the cultural landscape in your church and community.

It is undeniable that our language and culture are the lenses which help us to see the world and our place in it. Thankfully, we serve a God who transcends all barriers and who is the ultimate architect of the gifts of language, culture, and diversity. The beauty of our differences is by God's design, and we honor our Creator when we honor the languages and cultures of those that God has placed in our lives.

---

8. Storti, *The Art of Crossing Cultures*, 85.

Chapter 6 Reflection Questions

1. What is my cultural background? How does it affect the ways that I see the world?
2. What are some ways that I can better work with students who come from a different cultural background than I do?
3. Think about any students in your group that may not be native English speakers. What ideas in this chapter are most helpful to increase their learning?
4. What unique issues should I consider when working with refugee students and their families?
5. What third-culture kids and families are in our church? How can we better connect with and serve them?

7

Poverty and Trauma

"The Spirit of the Lord is on me, because he has anointed me to proclaim good news to the poor." Luke 4:18 NIV (quoting Isaiah 61:1)

IF YOU ASKED ME what some of the most heartbreaking issues were that I struggled with as a new teacher, poverty and trauma would be at the top of my list. Growing up in a middle-class home, I knew that my parents carefully budgeted and there was not always money for the latest trendy fashions or a newer car. But, there was never a time when I involuntarily missed a meal because the cupboards were empty, worried about whether or not our heat would work in the winter, feared being kicked out of our house, or experienced discrimination because of the color of my skin. I always knew that my home was a safe place, and I never had to question whether my basic needs would be met, or if my parents would love and support me.

One of the first important realizations I had in my classroom was that not every student came from the same background that I did. My first teaching job was at an affluent middle school where most parents faithfully attended parent-teacher conferences. There were always plenty of resources and support at home to create fancy, shiny posters and projects and finish daily homework on time. My students always had the school supplies they needed, and the only time they did not have a book or a coat was because they had forgotten it at home or in the car on the way to school.

Then, I moved to a high-poverty high school. Almost all of the students in my remedial English classes had after school jobs where they worked late into the night to help their family pay for rent, or they were responsible at home to care for younger siblings or elderly relatives while their parents worked. Riding the bus to school was their only option, and school was a place where they knew that breakfast and lunch were guaranteed every school day. My first year there, the mother of one of my students died from eating a diseased chicken they had butchered, and because of her undocumented status, they did not seek medical treatment for fear of deportation.

This section of the book is dedicated to those students and all that they taught me. Their names, stories, and faces are forever etched in my memory. I am sure that I learned far more from them than they ever learned from me.

Basic Understandings

In her book *A Framework for Understanding Poverty*, now in its sixth edition,[1] Ruby Payne divides poverty into two groups—situational and generational. Situational poverty can be considered more temporary. This type of poverty is usually due to an event which significantly disrupts the family financially, like divorce, job loss, sickness, natural disaster, business failure, etc. Generational poverty is defined as being in poverty for two generations or longer.

Payne defines poverty as the extent to which an individual goes without resources. Not every resource is necessarily tied to money. These are the additional resources she asserts can influence achievement: Emotional, mental/cognitive, spiritual, physical, support systems, role models, knowledge of hidden rules, language/

---

1. Payne, *A Framework for Understanding Poverty*, 10-12.

formal register. You can dig much deeper into each of these factors, but look back at the list of eight resources and note how many of them the church may be able to assist with. While you cannot necessarily influence a family's financial state, how much of a role can your church play in building a child's emotional and spiritual state? How might your church provide support systems and role models for students that can be consistent over time, especially when other adults in their life come and go?

Another key focus of Payne's research is the unwritten rules of each social class. Hidden rules are often unspoken, but they dictate how we tend to see the world function in it. For example, one of the most important middle-class rules is that work and achievement are driving forces in decision making. In generational poverty, survival, entertainment, and relationships are often the key driving forces. This is why one of your students may have a nicer cell phone than you do, but the inability to pay rent. Here are a few more examples of hidden class rules stated by Payne...[2]

Generational Poverty	Middle Class	Wealth
The "world" is most often defined in local terms.	The "world" is most often defined in national terms.	The "world" is most often defined in international terms.
Food is valued for its quantity.	Food is valued for its quality.	Food is valued for its presentation.
Laughter, when being disciplined, is a way to save face. Discipline is about penance and forgiveness, not change.	Reprimands are taken seriously without smiling and with respect toward authority. Discipline is about changing behavior.	Discipline may be carried out by those in the child's life other than the parents (nanny, tutor, etc.).

---

2. Payne, "Understanding and Working with Students and Adults from Poverty," 3.

Generational Poverty	Middle Class	Wealth
Physical fighting is how most conflict is resolved.	Fighting is usually verbal. Physical fighting is discouraged.	Fighting is done through lawyers and social inclusion and exclusion.
Destiny and fate govern. Because relationships are paramount, too much education is feared because the individual might leave.	Choice is key. Formal education is crucial for future success.	Education is for the purpose of social, financial, and political connections.

Keep in mind that these are all generalizations and not "one-size-fits-all" rules. They are based on patterns, and not stereotypes. All patterns have exceptions. However, thinking about the unwritten rules of a social class may help you better understand why a student or parent behaves or reacts in a certain way. Students living in poverty are no less capable or intelligent, and in some ways their "street smarts" may far exceed yours.

In my secondary English classroom, considering hidden class rules helped me better frame the literature and technical documents I taught using examples that my students could better understand. Reading a novel, poem, or play just because it is a literary classic and all educated people should understand its references made little difference to my students. But when we read *Romeo and Juliet* through the lens of two families who do not get along, the role of fate and timing, and the danger of impulsivity, suddenly, the story came alive to many of my students for the first time.

One of Payne's key points is that hidden rules can, and should, be discussed and learned, because their understanding can help students be more successful in different environments. For example, if a student laughs at you when reprimanded at church, they may be simply repeating the hidden rules that are in place at home. Helping the student understand that there is a set of unwritten middle-class rules that will bring success at church, school, and work, will help them build the cognitive structures necessary for learning. If an employee laughs at his boss when being reprimanded, he will probably be fired!

Another major difference between classes can often be the use of the casual and formal register. Casual register is based on a limited vocabulary (400-500 words) and broken sentence structure. It may include slang and dialects specific to a certain region or social group. This would be considered "playground language" or less formal conversations. Formal register is what we most often find in professional settings and academic writing. Students living in generational poverty spend the majority of their time in the casual register. Adults may find their language or tone disrespectful, especially in a disciplinary situation at school or church where it does not seem like a student is being serious enough. Helping students understand that their language and tone should change depending on their audience (informal vs. formal settings) and the subject matter (casual or serious), helps them to be able to more successfully navigate between classes and sometimes even different age groups.

Students who are living in generational poverty benefit greatly from direct teaching in this area so they can better understand when the hidden rules may be different from what they have always known and seen. If the hidden rules of the middle class are taught, students then have the understanding and ability to follow them if they wish. Being aware of hidden rules also helps church volunteers and pastors understand why a family may make decisions in a certain way that seems counter-productive, based on the norms of a different social class.

When individuals who have made it out of generational poverty are interviewed, virtually all reference an individual or individuals who made a significant difference for them. God has placed you in this position for a reason and greater purposes, and you may just be that one who God uses to change the trajectory of that child's life! People at your church from all walks of life can support children, teens, and adults to build resources, patterns of learning, and behaviors that may help them exit poverty.

Free and Reduced Lunch

Public k-12 schools use a federal formula to determine if a student qualifies for free and reduced lunch through the National School Lunch Program (NSLP). The calculations are based on the size of the family and the maximum income each year. Students eligible for free lunch typically live in a family which has an income less than 130% of the federal poverty level; students eligible for reduced lunch prices typically have a family income of less than 185% of the poverty level.[3] In fiscal year 2022, 30.1 million students, over 60% of all students in public schools in the United States, received a free or reduced-price lunch (FRL) through the NSLP.

So why is FRL eligibility important to your children's or youth program? Schools use FRL eligibility to determine the poverty level of the homes for the students that they serve. Often schools qualify for additional federal funding, support staff, or teacher loan forgiveness if they have a high population of students who are living in poverty. It is a federal requirement that FRL percentages be available online for all public k-12 schools, so it is easy information to access to determine the poverty level in your local community.

In your church, FRL eligibility is simply an easy way to better understand the income level of the students that you serve and if they may need financial assistance to participate in some of your activities. If you have students in your program that are attending public schools, they will usually know if they are eligible. While you would never want to call them out in front of their peers to check on their status, having a quick check box on the information sheet that they fill out each year or having a brief side conversation with a student or parent asking about their eligibility can give you a helpful reference on ways to better serve that family.

---

3. County Health Rankings, *Children Eligible for Free or Reduced-Price Lunch*.

McKinney-Vento Programs

The McKinney-Vento Homeless Assistance Act[4] provides a federal definition for the types of situations in which children and youth may be considered homeless. It has helped schools to broaden their classification of homeless students beyond just the lack of a regular residence to include students who share the housing of other persons or with multiple families (including grandparents), students whose parents are migrants, students who are living in shelters, campgrounds, or hotels, or children and youth living in cars, parks, public spaces, etc.

Under McKinney-Vento, students are entitled to a free, appropriate education even if they do not have a permanent address. They can enroll in school even if they do not have all of the required documents, and if they are in a situation where they move around a lot, the school can provide transportation to and from the school of origin, if requested.

Each public-school district has an appointed McKinney-Vento liaison. It may be helpful for your church's children and youth pastors to meet with this person to learn about what resources are available and what the level of need is for homeless students within the district. While some federal funding is available to schools who serve homeless students, usually the need is far greater than the resources available. While healthy food is always needed, families may also have limited access to health and hygiene items (soap, toothpaste, laundry detergent, deodorant, feminine products, etc.).

If the issue of homelessness has not already directly affected your church, there may be some powerful ministry opportunities just waiting for you in this area. Our church worked with our local police department to become a designated safe haven for families who need a place to sleep in their cars overnight. This led to two families in the community asking to park and live in their motorhomes in our church parking lot while they waited for an income check at the end of the month or space to open at a local campground.

---

4. McKinney-Vento Homeless Assistance Act, 42 US Code §§11431-11435.

Because they had-school aged children, McKinney-Vento funds from our local district paid for a temporary porta potty for the families to use after hours which was placed behind the church. These were temporary situations which were carefully overseen by the church board and school district, but were a tangible way that our church could help some "neighbors" in our community.

Factoring Costs

Take a minute and fill in the blank for every activity that is available to the students in your program *at a cost to them or their family*. Estimate how much each one costs in one year.

Church Camp: _____

Weekend Retreats: _____

Mission Trips: _____

Costumes for fall events, skits/plays, dress up days: _____

Gas required for off-site events where church transportation is not provided: _____

Group meals or snacks (i.e. ice cream) after an event: _____

Vacation Bible School Fee(s): _____

Childcare costs (when parents attend a church event where it is not provided): _____

Book fees for small groups: _____

White elephant or Secret Santa gifts for Christmas Party: _____

"Bring a snack to share" costs: _____

Music concerts attended as a group: _____

Entrance fees (roller skating, corn mazes, mini golf, etc.): _____

Dressy clothes for concerts or programs: _____

Group t-shirts or hoodies: _____

Data costs when registrations are required online: _____

Other: _____

Other: _____

TOTAL: _____

Were you surprised by the annual cost when you added it all up? Now, consider how many of your students also have at least one sibling in the program and multiply that total by the number of kids. How might pricing for participation affect families in your church experiencing poverty?

Often, students who do not have the money to participate will not sign up or show up to events or activities which cost extra money. This creates a divide between the "haves" and "have-nots" in your program. It could potentially further alienate the students from each other because they do not have as many opportunities for shared experiences.

It is vital to note here that most churches are on limited budgets and not everything can be free, but it may be helpful to think about the issue of expenses in the light of equality vs. equity. If you charge an equal amount to each student, everyone pays the exact same thing. However, equity is the recognition that each person has different circumstances and allocates the resources needed to reach an equal outcome. If families can pay full price for church camp, by all means, they should! But if cost is the only thing standing in the way for a student to attend church camp, how can your church help fill the gap? What might you do to make it a more equitable situation?

Providing fundraising opportunities like a car wash, yard sale, bake sale, etc. where students can earn money for their church account is one option often used. The more students (and their parents) work, the more money they can individually raise. It is important to offer a caution here because as effective as opportunities like this can be for some, your students who are living in poverty may not have items to donate, extra time to spare, or a grandmother willing to buy tubs of cookie dough or Christmas wreaths. As students get older, they can also feel embarrassed by their family's financial situation, so even if you offer a blanket statement on your advertising that says, "Scholarships available," they might be hesitant to ask for help. As you get to know your students better and understand their individual circumstances, it may be most helpful if you approach the student quietly, or call or send a text or email, and let them know that there is some money available for them to attend. You will get a higher response rate if you contact students individually as needed.

It is also important to remember the generosity available through your church family. Might there be some new empty nesters or seniors in your church who have the resources available to sponsor a student or an event? Many times, if members of your church are aware of a specific need (whether you mention the student's name or not), they are happy, and often eager, to help. Never underestimate the generous folks who fill the pews all around your students. It is a beautiful picture of the body of Christ!

Action Steps

Some of the most significant risk factors affecting children raised in poverty include emotional and social challenges, acute and chronic stressors, cognitive lags, and health and safety issues. Eric Jensen, in his book *Teaching with Poverty in Mind*, addresses how poverty can affect behavior and academic performance for students. Jensen states children being raised in poverty are more likely to display the following:

- Acting-out behaviors
- Impatience and impulsivity
- Gaps in politeness and social graces
- A more limited range of behavioral responses

- Inappropriate emotional responses
- Less empathy for others' misfortunes[5]

These behaviors can often cause great frustration for pastors and church volunteers who have less experience working with students who are living in poverty. However, it is essential that we do not label, demean, or blame students. Responses like cooperation, patience, empathy, gratitude, and forgiveness are learned responses that should be taught and demonstrated.

Jensen offers some practical and effective action steps that adults can implement in their work with children and teens whose lives have been affected by poverty. He states the following:

1. Embody respect. (Give it even when the student has not earned it.)
2. Share decision making.
3. Offer choice and gather input.
4. Avoid sarcasm.
5. Model adult thinking.
6. Keep your voice calm and controlled.
7. Discipline through positive relationships, not by power plays.
8. Teach basic meet-and-greet skills.
9. Remind students to thank their peers and adult helpers after collaborative activities.
10. Use inclusive language like "our church" and "our class."
11. Thank students for big and small things.
12. Celebrate effort and achievement.
13. Include acknowledgements and celebrations into every session.[6]

---

5. Jensen, *Teaching with Poverty in Mind*, 19.
6. Jensen, *Teaching with Poverty in Mind*, 21-22.

The Bible is loaded with examples of how an encounter with Christ or one of his followers dramatically changed someone's life. As we teach our students how to live out the teachings of Jesus, we are not only pointing them toward heaven, but we are showing them in big and small ways how to be God's image bearers right now on earth and to respond by following his example! Nothing is more powerful than teaching about appropriate emotional responses with Jesus as the primary instructor.

Social Capital

Opportunity Insights, a non-partisan, not-for-profit organization at Harvard University, published a study in 2022 analyzing the social capital of different socioeconomic levels using an online social network platform.[7] The group analyzed data on more than one billion friendship connections on Facebook and found that social networks tend to be segregated by income. Higher income people tend to have higher income friends. People in the bottom 10 percent socioeconomically have only two percent of friends that come from the top tier.

Why mention this study as part of this chapter? Consider how many jobs or opportunities you have been given not necessarily because of *what* you knew, but because of *who* you knew. The Opportunity Insights study spotlights the fact that people who grow up low-income in more economically connected counties tend to have higher earnings as adults. The more our communities are socioeconomically integrated, the more educational, social, and financial opportunities children and teens living in poverty may have.

Now put that in a church context. If we think of intergenerational church ministries where students of all backgrounds can form lasting quality relationships with a diverse group of people at church and expand their social networks, it could literally be life changing! The body of Christ working effectively can help reduce

---

7. Chetty, "Social Capital and Economic Mobility," 1-5.

the harm of poverty. The purpose of going to church is by no means to gain social capital, but it could be a beautiful by-product of the mysterious ways that God works.

As you think about the students that you work with and how many of them may be living in generational or situational poverty, never forget that our savior chose to come to earth as a pauper and be raised in a family with little means and societal standing. Our king could have been born in a palace, surrounded by every luxury imaginable, but he chose a stable. Jesus identifies with those who are poor and economically oppressed. In the gospels, he treats the poor with respect and dignity. May we, as his church, find ways to do the same.

Trauma

Just like poverty, trauma can literally rewire a person's brain. There are four ways in which we experience trauma: Directly, watching something happen to someone else, hearing about something that happened to someone else, or repeated exposure to a stressful experience. Rice and Groves define trauma as, " . . . an exceptional experience in which powerful and dangerous events overwhelm a person's capacity to cope."[8]

As someone who works in a church or a para-church organization, you will be in the trauma business, whether you want to be or not. Trauma is no respecter of age, gender, race, country of origin, socioeconomic status, or faith background. It can be destructive, controlling, and more damaging the longer it is left untreated, and often, unidentified. What you can control as a pastor or volunteer is what you do about it.

The research available on identifying and combating trauma has accelerated in the last 25 years and the education and mental health communities have learned much more about how to work with kids who have experienced trauma or traumatic episodes. *The American Journal of Preventive Medicine* published a

---

8. Rice, *Hope and Healing: Helping Young Children Affected by Trauma*, 3.

groundbreaking study in 1998 which started the discussion around a term referred to as ACE–Adverse Childhood Experiences. Using a 10-question survey, the study analyzed whether there was a relationship between childhood exposure to household dysfunction and emotional, physical, or sexual abuse and health risk behavior and disease in adulthood. More than half of the almost 10,000 respondents reported at least one adverse childhood experience. Participants who had experienced four or more categories of childhood exposure (compared to those who had none) had increased health risks for alcoholism, drug abuse, depression, and suicide attempts as adults. Those that scored higher on the seven categories of adverse childhood experiences were much more likely to have experienced heart disease, cancer, lung disease, skeletal fractures, and liver disease as they aged.[9]

The first ACE Study focused on factors at home (psychological, physical, or sexual abuse, violence against mother, living with household members who were substance abusers, mentally illness, or imprisonment). That research has more recently expanded to include community factors such as access to education and health care, historical trauma by an ethnic or cultural group, and intergenerational trauma (like generational poverty). The third realm of environmental factors includes natural disasters and pandemics.[10]

Many doctors' offices have incorporated an ACE screening as part of the intake process to get an idea of what life was like for the patient prior to their 18th birthday. If you have never taken an ACE survey, a quick internet search will give you access to a free questionnaire which will only take about three minutes to complete. Beginning to understand your own lived childhood experiences and how they may have affected you then and later in life is the first step to becoming trauma-informed.

---

9. Felitti, "Relationship of Childhood Abuse and Household Dysfunction," 245-58.

10. Sadin, *Trauma-Informed Teaching and IEPs: Strategies for Building Student Resilience*, 2.

Kristin Souers and Pete Hall, in their book *Fostering Resilient Learners: Strategies for Creating a Trauma Sensitive Classroom*, state these important truths about trauma:

1. Trauma is real.
2. Trauma is prevalent and more common than we usually realize.
3. Trauma is toxic to the brain and can affect learning and development in many different ways.
4. Schools [and churches] need to be prepared to support students who have experienced trauma.
5. Children are resilient and in supportive environments, they can learn, grow, and succeed.[11]

Children and adolescents who are living in survival mode will most often respond to stressful situations around them by withdrawing (flight), acting out (fight), or going numb (freeze). Sourers and Hall[12] list the following examples of what it might look like in your classroom or small group:

Flight	Fight	Freeze
• Withdrawing	• Acting out	• Exhibiting numbness
• Fleeing the room	• Behaving aggressively	• Refusing to answer
• Skipping class	• Acting silly	• Refusing to get help
• Daydreaming	• Exhibiting defiance	• Staring
• Pretending to sleep	• Being hyperactive	• Feeling unable to move or act
• Avoiding others	• Arguing	• Being unresponsive
• Hiding or wandering	• Screaming/yelling	
• Becoming disengaged		

---

11. Souers, *Fostering Resilient Learners*, 10-11.
12. Souers, *Fostering Resilient Learners*, 29.

One of the most important things that your staff and volunteers can do to become more trauma-sensitive is to shift your perspective from looking at unwanted and difficult behaviors as simply isolated, controllable actions on the part of the child, teen, or adult. As you get to know your students better and consider whether trauma may be a factor in their behaviors, you may discover that the behaviors you are seeing are simply their way of coping with traumatic experiences in their past or present. Consider these common behaviors compiled by Kathleen Guarino at the Institute of Educational Sciences[13] and what they could really be through a trauma-informed lens:

Traditional Perspective	Trauma-Informed Perspective
Manipulative	Getting needs met in ways that have worked in the past. Doing whatever is necessary to survive.
Lazy	Overwhelmed. Undeveloped executive functioning skills.
Resistant	Mistrustful of others due to a history of being hurt by others. Scared to make progress and then lose everything.
Unmotivated	Depressed, fearful, overwhelmed, frozen.
Disrespectful	Feeling threatened, unsafe, or out of control.
Attention-seeking	Feeling disconnected, alone, or unheard by others. Looking for connection.

Not every unwanted behavior that you see may be the result of trauma, but keeping it in the back of your mind as a factor may give you some potential root causes for the behaviors you are seeing in some students. But even if you are able to identify trauma as a possible factor, what does that mean for you and your program?

13. Guarino, "Trauma-Sensitive Practices in Schools," 4.

As workers in the church, you are not trained therapists! First, understand your limitations and understand that it is not all up to you to solve things for your students. However, you can analyze your programs and programming through a trauma-sensitive lens and understand the impact that trauma can have. As you ensure emotional and physical safety for your students, your relationship with them can be part of their healing process. Some of these simple practices previously discussed can help make your church environment a safe place for your students. Guarino states these key practices that can be quickly implemented:

- Clear expectations posted, stated, and reinforced
- Neat and orderly physical space that is well lit and well monitored
- Adult responses are calm and respectful
- Choice and empowerment are encouraged
- Positive behaviors are praised and reinforced
- A quiet place is available if students feel overwhelmed or out of control
- Triggers are reduced whenever possible[14]

Consider this scenario . . . During Holy Week, your youth group meets on Wednesday night to watch an epic biblical drama which portrays the crucifixion and resurrection. You rent a projector so the screen can literally fill the entire front of the youth room. You have to begin a little early and go a little late so there is time to watch the entire movie. You want to make the experience as real as possible, so you rearrange the furniture, use surround sound speakers, and shut off all of the lights. At one point as the movie has just begun, you can see police lights out of the church window from the street below. You quickly close the blinds so it does not disrupt the movie. Later, during the crucifixion scene, you are expecting students to be moved by what they experience, but you were shocked by the responses of two of your students.

14. Guarino, "Trauma-Sensitive Practices in Schools," 7-9.

Will, a junior new to the youth group, ran out of the room and out of the church building. A youth worker tried to follow him and make sure that he was okay, yelling his name several times, but he did not ever turn around or attempt to talk. He went straight to his car and drove away. At the same time that this was happening, Alejandra, a freshman, started throwing popcorn at the student in front of her and kept laughing and making inappropriate noises at one of the most important parts of the movie. What is wrong with these kids? Why could they just not sit quietly and watch the movie?

The most likely answer for what just happened is that Will and Alejandra have experienced trauma in the past and elements of the environment and the movie caused their bodies to react as if the trauma was happening again at that moment to them. The behaviors they just experienced are connected to the flight (Will) and fight (Alejandra) reactions. They were not being rude; they were in survival mode!

Look at the scenario again and see how many of these common triggers for trauma victims were present during your movie night. Guarino provides this research-based checklist:

- Loud, chaotic environments
- Physical touch, uncertainty about expectations, or changes in routine
- Hand or body gestures that appear threatening
- Witnessing violence between others
- Particular reminders about an event (weather, time of year, smells)
- Emergency vehicles and police or fire personnel
- Areas of the building that are experienced as unsafe, such as bathrooms or less well-monitored areas[15]

While the youth pastor did not intend for the setting and the movie to be a trigger for some of his students, it definitely may

15. Guarino, "Trauma-Sensitive Practices in Schools," 11.

have been. So, does that mean that you can never watch a powerful movie or rearrange the furniture? No. However, what if the following elements were adjusted in this scenario:

1. The week before, the pastor shared with the students what would be happening the next Wednesday night. A handout was provided for students to take home which discussed the movie and the violence portrayed so it was clear what they would be viewing. Parents were given the opportunity to screen it ahead of time.

2. Students were given the opportunity to opt out and be part of a different activity that night if they did not want to watch the video.

3. When students entered the room, all of the lights were on at first. The pastor asked if it was okay to dim the lights or if students preferred that they stayed on.

4. The pastor experimented ahead of time with the volume to make sure that it is not too loud. One student was reminded to bring his noise-canceling headphones to wear if the more intense scenes got too loud for him.

5. Before starting the movie, the pastor shared that there are some scenes in the movie which include anguish, betrayal, and torture. He explained that these can be really difficult to watch and they can elicit some strong emotions. "It is very normal to feel this way when you watch these scenes." On the side board is the list of the most difficult scenes and about how long they last (2 minutes, 5 minutes, etc.) "If what you see is disturbing to you, it is okay to move to the back of the room, go get a drink, or wait in the quiet room for as long as you need to. Miss Dana will be at the back and is available to stand out in the hall and talk with you or take a walk if you need one."

6. Youth workers are spread out around the room and instructed to watch the body language of the students and be aware of their emotional state during the video.

7. When the police lights can be seen out the window, the pastor looks outside and lets the students know it is just a routine traffic stop, and then closes the blinds.

8. The pastor purposely cuts out some slower scenes to provide more discussion time at the end. This way he can make sure that students have the opportunity to discuss what they have watched and how it made them feel before they leave.

These ideas for minor changes could have made all of the difference for Will and Alejandra. While we cannot fix anything that has happened to our students in the past, we can certainly help them in the present.

The Regional Educational Laboratory (REL) Programs, through the U.S. Department of Education, offer the following "in the moment" strategies when working with kids who are reliving past trauma or are in a current crisis:

Safe and Predictable Environment: Be aware of the student's body language, tone of voice, and emotional state. Direct other students to follow outlined safety procedures when necessary. Provide the student with the opportunity to go to a safe space if needed and alert appropriate support staff and/or caregivers.

Relationship Building: Project calmness both verbally and non-verbally. Use a gentle voice and position yourself next to them instead of standing over or directly facing. Show you are interested and fully present with them in the moment. Express your care for the student and their safety.

Self-Regulation: Relax before you respond (deep breath, count to 10, etc.). Encourage the student to use their own relaxation and coping skills, as well as comfort objects when available. Validate their emotions by stating what you see. "You seem frustrated right now. Is that correct?" Assist the student in identifying reasonable and safe response options (quiet room, taking a walk, etc.).[16]

16. Institution of Education Sciences, "Common Trauma Symptoms in Students and Helpful Strategies for Educators," 2.

When a student is in crisis, do not argue or get into a power struggle. Keep your tone calm and do not raise your voice or yell. Whenever possible, do not handle the situation in front of peers or use punitive punishment.

After the crisis has subsided, it is important to follow up with the student and help them debrief what happened. (This will also be helpful for you!) Find a safe place to talk about what happened. Praise the student for any coping or relaxation skills they used. Discuss possible consequences if the behavior continues and identify specific steps needed for resuming participation. These may need to be in writing, depending on the severity. It will also be beneficial for you to document what happened and how you responded for future reference.

As we end this chapter, it is helpful to conclude with the reminder that helping students grasp the physical, emotional, and spiritual sufferings of Jesus and what he endured on the cross is a powerful reminder that we have a savior who truly understands pain and trauma! He knows what our students are going through and is the only one who can truly be an ever-present help in times of need.

Chapter 7 Reflection Questions

1. How do the issues of poverty and trauma affect the way that my students see themselves and their place in the world?
2. What social class hidden rules stand out to me the most? How might this inform my work with students from a different social class than my own?
3. What are some of the most important things to remember when working with students in poverty or who have experienced trauma?
4. Reflect on the life and ministry of Jesus Christ. How did he specifically respond to the poor and broken that he encountered?

8

Depression and Anxiety

"I have told you these things, so that in me you may have peace. In this world you will have trouble. But take heart! I have overcome the world." John 16:33 NIV

MENTAL HEALTH STRUGGLES HAVE always existed in our society, but the COVID pandemic and social media have helped to intensify the issue to almost epidemic proportions. Teens can have hundreds or thousands of friends on social media yet feel constantly isolated and alone. They are the most connected generation in history, yet they can often feel disconnected, anxious, and afraid.

Since 1991, the Center for Disease Control and Prevention (CDC) has administered and compiled a Youth Risk Behavior Survey for high schoolers every two years. It is often disaggregated by state, and is a helpful resource for understanding some of the issues and trends that youth are wrestling with including sexual behavior, substance abuse, experiences of violence, mental health, and suicide ideation. The February 2023 release[1] showed that the rate of depression and anxiety among high school students

---

1. Centers for Disease Control and Prevention, *Youth Risk Behavior Survey 2023*.

is at an all-time high. Three in five teenage girls report feeling sad and depressed, an amount 60 percent higher than a decade ago. For boys, that number has risen from 21 percent to 27 percent. Of the females surveyed, 25 percent had contemplated suicide, and 10 percent had made at least one attempt. That is a staggering one in 10 high school girls! Now, consider what that statistic might mean for the number of females in your church group. While the CDC's study does not disaggregate responses based on identified faith preferences, we know that churches are not immune or exempt, and it is likely that this subject has touched you and your community very close to home.

As we begin this chapter, it is very important to reiterate that pastors and volunteers in the church are not trained counselors or therapists. (If you do happen to have a few in your congregation, they can be tremendous resources for you!) *Do not* feel like you have to solve or fix issues of mental health for your students. Unless you truly are an expert, then do not ever place that responsibility or expectation upon yourself, even for a minute. God has placed you in the lives of your students to be an encouraging and supportive adult who can walk alongside them on good days and on difficult days. As you will read about in the next chapter, often they need someone who will simply listen more than speak. Be available. Let them know you care. Never feel like it is your job to heal or mend a student's struggles. Only God can do that, and often God uses professionals who specialize in mental health and medication to help children, teens, and adults rebuild their lives.

If you do have students in your groups at church who are struggling with depression and anxiety and are not receiving treatment, consider working with trusted members of your church and community to create a referral list of Christian counselors in your area that are known for their care and effectiveness. This is a very helpful resource to have on hand to share with parents when needed. Many insurance companies provide a limited number of free counseling sessions through their Employee Assistance Program (EAP). Most schools also have professional school counselors, but often their caseloads are quite large and they are not always able to meet with students on a regular basis. However, they can be a very good starting place. School counselors and classroom teachers see students on a daily basis and are often the first to notice changes. If your community contains a college or university which offers master's degrees in counseling or social work, they may have a counseling center staffed by interns which operates on a sliding scale for families who have limited financial resources. If you are not already aware of the counseling options in your community, this is a good time to begin investigating what is available.

Depression

You only have to spend about five minutes with a group of teenagers to witness how volatile emotions and interests can be at that age. That is why depression can be a tricky road to navigate because things are already changing so quickly. However, counselors and psychologists tend to use the term "persistent" when diagnosing depression because it is ongoing, not fleeting like emotions can be in adolescence. Depression interferes with the activities of daily life (sleeping, eating, hygiene) and can rob students of energy and the desire to participate in hobbies or activities that they once loved.

While depression can manifest itself in different ways and at different times, these are some typical indicators that a student might be depressed if they occur over time:

- Anger or irritability, even over things that seem trivial
- Prolonged feelings of sadness, hopelessness, guilt, and/or helplessness
- Loss of interest or pleasure in usual activities
- Poorer academic performance, including absenteeism
- Changes in sleeping or eating habits (Typically sleeping a lot more and eating a lot more or a lot less)
- Experimentation with drugs or alcohol as a means to escape or numb the pain

- Trouble concentrating
- Lack of typical hygiene routines (not bathing, changing clothes, combing hair, etc.)
- At the most extreme points of clinical depression, the person has no strength or energy to even get out of bed.[2]

What can you do for a student in your church group who is experiencing depression?

1. Talk with the student directly. Ask them how they are managing their feelings and challenges. (This is much easier to do after you have already built a relationship with the student.)
2. Find big and small ways to increase the social support and sense of connectedness provided within your youth group by both the students and adults. How can students stay connected to you and each other beyond just Sunday morning and Wednesday night?
3. Model and promote positive coping skills: Physical activity, encouraging music, healthy eating, water consumption, sleeping at least eight hours a night, restricted social media time, creativity through art, journaling, or fellowship.
4. Encourage conversations within the home between parents and children. Provide follow-up questions after a lesson that can be discussed on the way home from church or during the week.
5. Be aware of things happening within the community, school, or family which might be distressing to your student. Sometimes current events or the loss of a loved one can intensify the depression that is already present. Reaching out mid-week with a note, phone call, or text can be very powerful.[3]

---

2. Centers for Disease Control, *Anxiety and Depression in Children*.
3. Lee, "Mental Health Concerns for Teenagers Post-COVID," 1.

It is encouraging to note that students who have a positive, active life of faith are 60 percent less likely to use and abuse substances and are 80 percent less likely to be depressed as teenagers.[4] Clinical psychologist Dr. Lisa Miller, in her book *The Spiritual Child: The New Science on Parenting for Health and Lifelong Thriving*, offers the following guidance on how adults can help teens feel that they are a valuable member of their world and grasp how they contribute to a bigger story:

1. Provide transparency in our own spiritual lives. Narrate our own spiritual practices for our kids (personal prayer, devotions, worship, etc.).
2. Model empathy. How can we tangibly lend a hand to an individual or group in need?
3. Start spiritual traditions within the home.
4. Use questions to open lifelong conversations. (How are you feeling about . . . ?) Admit when you do not have the answer.
5. Help children find their inner spiritual compass that points to the truth. Call attention to good behaviors and point out how the Holy Spirit may have been working in that situation.
6. Foster spiritual development and encourage opportunities for students to make faith their own, even if the exploration feels uncomfortable.[5]

Social Media

According to the U.S. Surgeon General's Advisory in 2023[6], based on dozens of studies, 77 percent of our teens are on social media

---

4. Miller, *The Spiritual Child: The New Science on Parenting for Health and Lifelong Thriving*, 209.

5. Miller, *The Spiritual Child: The New Science on Parenting for Health and Lifelong Thriving*, 331–48.

6. U.S. Dept. of Health and Human Services, *Social Media and Youth Mental Health*.

daily, and just over half spend four or more hours on social media daily. The average is 4.8 hours. Most online platforms have a stated age of at least 13, but 40 percent of kids ages 8-12 are using them on a regular basis, sometimes with little or no oversight from their parents. Social media may also perpetuate eating disorders, body dissatisfaction, social comparison, and low self-esteem, especially among girls.

The advisory report offers several suggestions about what parents and caregivers can do to mitigate the harms of social media. Many can apply to the church or could be used to educate families in your congregation:

- Create a media plan which includes healthy technology boundaries at home, school, and church.
- Create tech-free zones and encourage children and youth to deepen in-person friendships.
- Model responsible social media behaviors both in modeling positive behavior online and monitoring time spent online.
- Talk with students often about their privacy settings, their online friendships and experiences, and how they are spending their time online. Questions like, "How are things going online?" are just as important as "How was your day?"
- Report cyberbullying and online exploitation. Open the door for conversations around these subjects within small groups.
- Establish parent support programs to help create shared norms and practices around healthy social media use.

Suicide

As a society, talking about suicide or asking a person if they feel suicidal is often the unmentionable subject, as though talking about it will make students start thinking about it. Actually, the opposite is true. A person who is experiencing extreme depression needs to be encouraged to share with a trusted adult what they are feeling and thinking about. Talking about suicide ideation provides an opportunity for communication and can be an opportunity for further assistance. If you are ever in this situation, ask the student what help they have already been receiving (counseling, support groups, etc.). How has it been working? Are they taking any medication for their symptoms, and did they remember to take it that day? If they are not receiving any professional help, brainstorm options for care. (Remember, a student experiencing depression may not be thinking clearly, so you may need to offer ideas for resources and follow-through to see if they have reached out.) Make sure that their parents or guardian is aware of the conversation.

Never promise a student that you will keep a secret. As a responsible adult, sometimes your role will require you to share information with parents or crisis personnel. It is best to always have a statement ready which goes something like this—"If you want to talk to me about harm to yourself or others, or if you share with me that you have been abused in some way, I am required by law to share that information to make sure you get the help that you need."

Pastors and volunteers working with adolescents in church settings need to keep their eyes and ears open for direct and indirect verbal cues, as well as behavioral cues, that might be an indicator that a student is contemplating suicide. While they can manifest differently for different students, any comments, behaviors, or actions are worth following up with the student and a parent. Suicide Awareness Voices of Education (SAVE), lists the following warning signs:

Direct Verbal Cues:

- Talking, reading, or writing about suicide or death.
- Talking about feeling worthless or helpless.

- Saying things like, "I'm going to kill myself," "I wish I were dead," "I'm going to end it all," or "If _____, doesn't (or does) happen, I'll kill myself."

Indirect Verbal Cues

- "What's the point of going on?"
- "My family would be better off without me."
- "Who cares if I am dead, anyway?"
- "I just want out; I am so tired of it all."
- "Soon, you won't have to worry about me."
- "You are going to regret how you have treated me."

Behavioral Cues

- Changes in behavior—irritability, withdrawing, eating or sleeping patterns.
- Giving away things or returning borrowed items.
- Self-destructive or other risk-taking behaviors.
- Experimentation with drugs or alcohol.
- Decreased interest in friends or hobbies.
- Any sudden "happiness" in someone who has been depressed.[7]

A student who tells you that they have a *suicide plan* and *access to means* (pills, firearms, ropes, high buildings, etc.) is much more likely to make an attempt. It is crucial that you act upon this information immediately and not send the student home, *unless* you are placing them directly in the care of a responsible parent or caregiver who is aware of the conversation and immediacy of the concern. Stay with the student until help can be found. The 9-8-8 suicide and crisis lifeline is a good number to add to your contacts on your phone right now. (In the moment,

---

7. Suicide Awareness Voices of Education (SAVE), "Warning Signs of Suicide."

you may not remember the number.) This could also be posted in your youth room and shared with your teen leaders. It is a free resource available 24 hours a day, in English, Spanish, and for the deaf and hard of hearing.

It is important to remember that just because a student is a Christian, they might not be spared from depression or suicide ideation. Students can still have deep pain even when they have deep faith. Often when students are in the depths of despair and unable to get out of bed, they can't even contemplate suicide because they are not fully functioning. It is only when they start to feel a little better that they have the mental and physical bandwidth to begin to make a plan to end their lives. For a student with clinical depression, the point at which they are starting to "come out of it" and seem a little more like themselves should actually be the point at which everyone is on high alert.

Reverend Rick Warren, author of *A Purpose Driven Life*, and his wife Kay, have been very open about losing their son, Matthew, to suicide in 2013. Four months after Matthew's death, as part of his first sermon after bereavement leave, Warren told his congregation, "For 27 years, I prayed every day of my life for God to heal my son's mental illness. It was the number one prayer of my life," he preached. "It just didn't make sense why this prayer was not being answered." He then went on to discuss the importance of removing the stigma around mental illness in the church and directly addressed those in his congregation who have struggled with it. "Your illness is not your identity; your chemistry is not your character." To their families, he said, "We are here for you, and we are in this together." There is hope for the future: "God wants to take your greatest loss and turn it into your greatest life message."[8]

The more churches can create and maintain non-judgmental spaces where adolescents can express their feelings and find emotional support and encouragement, the more we function as the true body of Christ in our world. Working with kids and teens

---

8. Dias, "Rick Warren Preaches First Sermon Since His Son's Suicide."

often means climbing into the trenches with them. The work is not easy, but it can be life-changing and sometimes lifesaving.

Anxiety and OCD

Workers in the church have a unique opportunity to watch kids grow and mature from one year to the next. Seeing students on a weekly basis over long periods of time puts us in a strategic place to live life together, share grief, and celebrate accomplishments. It also means that pastors and volunteers may notice changes that may be of concern. Just as instances of depression are on the rise among our students, so is anxiety.

One of the first tools that a counselor will introduce to a student struggling with anxiety is breathing techniques. Intentional breathing is a powerful gift that God empowers us with to influence both our brain and autonomic nervous systems. If you have a student in your group that is struggling with anxiety, ask about what breathing techniques he or she is using that are working. It is another way you can connect and encourage. You might also learn a few that you want to try on your own!

Jennifer Tucker, in her book *Breath as Prayer*[9], offers some breathing techniques that are based directly on the words of scripture. The book can be read as a daily devotional, or you can use the table of contents to find a scripture and a breath prayer for a specific challenge or fear you are facing. While I was in the process of writing this book, I was diagnosed with a breast cancer recurrence and was practically knocked over by how quickly all of the fears and anxiety from my past cancer battle came flooding back. A dear friend gave me Tucker's book and the breath prayers were what I would practice over and over again as I endured 33 daily radiation treatments. We all have moments when we need to pray, but the words will just not come. Breath prayers helped me connect my brain and body with the power that is the Word of God. The radiation room became my

---

9. Tucker, *Breath as Prayer*.

prayer studio, and God met me there every day, calming my anxiety and filling me with his presence.

While it is common for all of us to have worry and fears at certain times and also find comfort in our routines and rituals, what makes anxiety disorders and obsessive-compulsive disorder (OCD) different is the intensity and frequency that they occur. Are the fears and behaviors getting in the way of everyday life? Does reason and common sense not serve to comfort or reassure? Can the fears or behavior be stopped or interrupted at will? Are the fears typical for the age group and experiences of the student? Do the fear and behaviors consume an inordinate amount of time? Are the behaviors distressing or overwhelming? These may be some indicators that the issues are more pervasive than what is typical and the student may need specialized help.[10]

The following are some possible signs and symptoms of anxiety disorders that may be observable in school and church settings:

- Student appears overly cautious, nervous, shy, or fearful.
- Student may constantly be seeking approval or reassurance.
- Fears may be expressed by crying or throwing tantrums (especially for younger students). Once emotions are heightened, it may be very difficult for them to calm down.
- Physical symptoms may exist like stomach aches, rapid heartbeat, pounding headache, difficulty breathing, excessive sweating, or shaking.
- Students may experience full panic episodes or attacks.

OCD is a combination of obsessions (thinking) and compulsions (behavior). Obsessions can include repeated thoughts about something (germs, dying, bad things happening, doing something wrong) and can even be as severe as disturbing or unwanted thoughts about hurting others or things of a sexual nature. (Important note: Students with OCD who have violent or sexual thoughts find those thoughts to be very upsetting. This

10. Adams, *Students with OCD: A Handbook for School Personnel*, 10–11.

does not mean that they have any desire to act upon them and should not be considered dangerous to others.)[11]

Compulsions are the behaviors that can accompany the thinking patterns. If a student is worried about germs, then he might wash his hands constantly or refuse to touch things that have been touched by others. A student worried about getting an answer wrong might constantly check or recheck answers, erase repeatedly, or cry when she has colored outside the lines. A student obsessing about forgetting something might rehearse letters, words, or sentences repeatedly. Students with bathroom OCD or toilet phobia might worry about not being able to get to the bathroom in time or have concerns about others hearing them use the restroom, so they may either take frequent trips to the bathroom or refuse to use a bathroom at church. Again, in each of these examples, a single isolated incident is not a compulsion. It is when the behavior takes place repeatedly—several times an hour or a day, every day. You might also notice things like frustration when things are disorganized or routines change, odd behaviors with walking patterns, counting, touching or tapping, or an excessive need for reassurance.

Just like other disabilities, if a child or teen's anxiety or OCD affects their performance at school, they may qualify for a 504 plan or IEP. Typical classroom accommodations revolve around a plan for the following fears: Contamination (washing and cleaning), doubting (reassurance seeking, over checking), and/or tardiness and procrastination. The first thing to acknowledge as a church is that the fears of that child or teen are real to them and may be out of their control. But the situation is not hopeless—professional help is available and, most likely necessary, for them to lead a normal life. With help, anxiety and OCD can be managed. The church's job is not to "fix" the diagnosis, but there are some easy things that can be done that will help the student feel more relaxed and welcomed. Here are some accommodations that might be helpful in your setting, adapted from recommendations by the International OCD Foundation:

11. International OCD Foundation, *Anxiety in the Classroom*.

Contamination Fears

- Allow the student to bring his own Bible or supplies (pencil, crayons, etc.) or have a Bible (or books or supplies) in the room that are only for his use.
- Seat the student where she will be the first one to receive handouts.
- Let the student be the first in line to get food or use the restroom or drinking fountain.
- Provide an easy out for the student to avoid activities where a lot of touching is involved. (Ex: serving as the scorekeeper or timekeeper)
- Keep hand sanitizer readily available.

Doubting

- Limit the number of open-ended options available.
- Check progress intermittently to offer encouragement and let the student know he is on the right track.
- Break larger tasks into more manageable segments.
- Make special allowances for memorization. (I.E. Allow the student to use a script for her part in the Christmas play or weekly Bible verse memory.)
- Provide a pencil without an eraser.

Self-Esteem and Social Issues

- Pre-arrange a signal that the student can use if he needs to leave the room when he is starting to feel overwhelmed. (Time limits for the break should be established in advance.)
- Seat the student in a location where her symptoms will be the least obvious to her peers.

- Do not try to stop a ritual when the student is exhibiting a high level of anxiety, but do direct the attention of classmates away from the student to prevent humiliation.
- Always interact calmly and in a reassuring manner with the student.
- Highlight the student's strengths and talents.
- Structure discussions and groupings by pairing the student with those who have a high level of empathy and respect.
- Avoid situations in which team captains choose teams or students choose their own groups. This often leads to the student with anxiety or OCD being left out, which can magnify their fears.
- Establish a buddy system in which certain empathetic students or adult helpers look out for kids who are isolating. Often no words even have to be said. Just the act of having someone "in your corner" is comforting.

Procrastination

- Allow tardiness. Avoid negative consequences because they tend to increase stress and anxiety. (Students with anxiety and OCD are actually more likely to arrive on time when they know that there will *not* be a penalty.)
- If the student arrives late, do not draw attention to the student and ignore their entrance as much as possible, minimizing their embarrassment in front of the group.[12]

While the topics of this chapter can be very disheartening, we cannot forget that our hope is found in Jesus Christ. The Bible shows us the full range of emotion that Jesus experienced as a man. Sometimes, just talking about the feelings and struggles that our "biblical superstars" experienced is a good way to open the door

---

12. International OCD Foundation, *Anxiety in the Classroom*.

to conversations about how that might apply to our own lives or what we can learn from them. The Bible does not gloss over challenges. They were just as real then as they are now, and we need to talk about them. But we also learn from those stories that we are created for community, and that community can be one means of helping us cope and heal. Rick Warren, in an interview with TBN about the loss of his son, said, "If I had not had a small group, I do not know if I would still be in ministry right now."[13] No matter what your students and their families are facing, may they always find support and encouragement within our churches.

Chapter 8 Reflection Questions

1. What are the signs and symptoms of depression? How about anxiety?
2. What red flags do I need to watch out for?
3. How can I be a caring adult in the life of a student if I am not a trained counselor?
4. What changes might I need to make in my program to help a student with anxiety be more successful?
5. How can our church positively support students and their parents if they struggle with any of these issues?

---

13. TBN, *Rick Warren Testimony: My Son Matthew's Suicide and How Ministry Flows from Deep Pain.*

9

Reflective Listening and Boundaries

"My dear brothers and sisters, take note of this: Everyone should be quick to listen, slow to speak and slow to become angry." James 1:19 NIV

AS YOU HAVE READ in previous chapters, the key to teaching and learning lies in the power of the relationship. It is the caring relationships from adults in your church that will point your students to Jesus and, as an added bi-product, will also most likely help them do better in school, lower drug and alcohol abuse rates, lower suicide rates, reduce their likelihood of entering the juvenile justice system, and promote stronger mental health. Why? Simply because they have at least one positive adult in their life that knows and cares about them.

As students begin to trust you, it is very likely that they will also confide more in you. A listening ear can be very therapeutic, and you do not have to be a trained counselor to be a good listener. This chapter will explore the keys to reflective listening along with some mandatory reporting laws and ethical boundaries that need to be in place in your church programming.

Listening Basics

Our culture is often very good at talking, but seldom good at really listening. Reflective listening is an art and a skill that can be improved with practice, patience, and compassion. If you want to strengthen your relationship with a student, or anyone else, for that matter, talk less and listen more. Becoming a better listener means putting the needs (and voice) of your student above your own. Proverbs 18:13 says, "He who answers before listening—that is his folly and shame." So how do you start becoming a reflective listener?

Ruth Hetzendorfer, in her book, *The Pastoral Counseling Handbook: A Guide to Helping the Hurting,* recommends starting the process by asking yourself these questions:

- Am I tuning in to what a person is saying, or am I relating it to myself?
- Am I assuming I know what a person is going to say and stop listening?
- Do I concentrate on the meaning of the message?
- Do I watch verbal and nonverbal behavior?
- Do I consider the best way to respond?
- Do I practice these skills with others to sharpen my ability to really hear what a person is saying?[1]

Once you have analyzed your own tendencies to jump in and try to fix things or believe that you have to have the "right answers," you are ready to start listening and follow the advice in the book of James to "be quick to listen and slow to speak."[2]

Begin by Validating. People have to be able to name and identify their pain to begin the healing process. Knowing that they are heard and understood by a trusted adult or friend helps them

---

1. Hetzendorfer, *The Pastoral Counseling Handbook: A Guide to Helping the Hurting,* 19.
2. James 1:19 NIV.

feel seen and supported. It is the difference between pushing or pulling someone along and truly walking alongside them as they journey through dark days or circumstances. Validation of feelings is crucial to the listening process. Even if you might feel or act differently if placed in the same situation, focus on what *they* are feeling and trying to express. (Remember, it is not about you!) Hetzendorfer suggests the following statements to help validate that what they are saying is important:

- "I can see that you feel hurt when you think about it."
- "It sounds like you have been in a lot of pain over this."
- "I can't imagine what you have been through."
- "I can see you are hurting."[3]

Paraphrase. Briefly restate in your own words the main message (or source of pain or brokenness) of what you just heard. After their feelings are validated, paraphrasing the main idea out loud back to them helps them know that you understood what they were saying. Typically, you paraphrase at several points during the conversation. It also keeps you engaged and in tune to what they are telling you. Paraphrasing should be phrased as a statement.

Examples: "I think that you are saying that . . . your mom's expectations keep changing, so you do not ever know where you stand with her." / "It sounds like . . . it was a really hard day at school today." / "So, you feel like . . . this task is impossible right now." / "You are concerned that . . . your friends are making some bad choices."

Clarify. This part of the process helps you make sure you understand them correctly. When students are processing emotions or struggling to find the right words to express what is going on, they themselves may not have all of the details clear in their minds, or they may not come out clearly when they try to talk about them. This is okay! Remember that as you listen, as long as you can understand the main idea or point of what they are saying, the minor

3. Hetzendorfer, *The Pastoral Counseling Handbook: A Guide to Helping the Hurting*, 20.

details are unimportant. Do not ask them to clarify something that is unclear unless it is an important detail. However, do provide a clarifying response or ask a clarifying question when it is a main idea or key point that you need to understand. Focus on what does not make sense in what they are telling you, or determine what additional information you need in order to better understand. Often you may need their help in connecting the dots.

Examples: "Can you give me an example of that?" / "You just said that [such and such] is important. Can you help me understand what that means to you?" / "If you do not care about this person, why does her opinion matter to you?" / "What do you think is getting in the way of your ability to make closer friends in the youth group?" / "It sounds like you are frustrated that you are not growing in your relationship with God, but you do not know what to do about it."

Reflective Feelings. At this point in the conversation, it is helpful to name the feelings that the student is sharing. It can bring some reflection on things that he or she has possibly not understood or realized about the situation. Hetzendorder suggests asking yourself the following questions at this stage:

- What is the overall feeling?
- What does the student's tone suggest?
- Is the student's body language saying something different from the words that they are using?[4]

Then, make sure that the student identifies that the feeling you have just named is correct. If you are off base, they will tell you.

Examples: "You seem to feel frustrated by what is going on at home. Do you always feel this way?" / "It really hurts when you are rejected by someone you care about. You seem very angry about what happened." / "You are laughing and smiling when you are with the group, but I can tell that you are trying to hide how

---

4. Hetzendorfer, *The Pastoral Counseling Handbook: A Guide to Helping the Hurting*, 22.

you really feel." / "You have been through a lot. It is okay to feel exhausted."

Also, remember that your tone and body language matters as much as theirs. The student may go through a range of emotions while talking to you, and just because they are upset or frustrated, it is helpful not to take it personally, even if they are frustrated at you, another adult, or another student or group of students. If you start to get defensive, even a little, their tension will escalate. Try not to cross your arms, as that closed position can act like a barrier sometimes. Nodding your head occasionally and inserting phrases to show that you are listening ("I see," "Uh-huh," "That makes sense," "I hear you," etc.) will serve as a reminder to the student that you are present and really hearing what they are saying. Remaining calm and collected will help de-escalate the situation and help to calm a student down if they are very emotional.

Finding a Stopping Place

You will most likely have two extremes in your group—students who you can't ever get to talk to you, and those who want to talk to you all of the time! As you build trust with students, they will be more open to sharing what is going on in their lives. However, you can't physically or logistically stay late every Wednesday night if a student always needs to talk. Determine what your parameters will be if you have a habitual talker who has no concept of time. It is okay, and important, to be upfront about how much time you have. For example, "I just have five minutes now, but if we need more time we can schedule an additional time to talk." I have a clock in my office on the wall just behind the chair that my students usually sit in when they come in to talk. This way I can keep glancing at the clock above their heads to know what time it is instead of always having to glance at my watch.

As you conclude the conversation, thank the student for trusting you enough to share. Ask them to summarize the results of the conversation (if applicable) and ask what follow-up would be helpful. Most importantly, assure them that you are available to talk again, and ask what other supportive adults they have in their lives at home, school, or church when they need help. Most students can easily list at least three or four adults that they can turn to when needed, but be on high alert when they are not easily able to list at least a few names. These are the students who will need some extra support from the pastors and adults at your church.

Disclosing Abuse

As a mandated reporter, legally, if a student discloses abuse (physical, sexual, or emotional) or shares that they intend to harm themselves or another person, you are required by the laws in your state to report that information to the authorities. These laws override confidentiality between pastors and their congregants. You should never state or even hint that you will keep a secret or promise "not to tell" something that has been shared with you. Being upfront with students about your requirement to report abuse or harm is part of your job as a caring adult.

If it ever becomes necessary to report abuse, most states have a 24-hour reporting window, which includes weekends. This means that if a student discloses something on Friday night, you will have until that same time on Saturday night to report it. Typically, you should call Child Protective Services (CPS) in your local area. They will ask for the student's address, birthdate, and as much information as you have regarding the identity of the alleged perpetrator. You are considered a confidential reporter, but your information could be disclosed if the case ever goes to court. There is no statute of limitations on abuse, so if a student discloses abuse that happened several years ago, you still must report it within the next 24 hours.

It is important to understand that your job as a mandatory reporter is not to be the judge and jury, but simply report what the student told you. There have been a few times in my work as a school counselor where I called CPS when it was an unusual situation and I was not sure if it should be reported or not. They were gracious to help me through it and each time assured me it was something that should be reported. Remember if a student is in immediate harm to self or others, or if it is not safe to go home, call 211 or 911 immediately.

Rick Warren said in an interview, "The deeper the pain, the fewer words you use . . . Show up and shut up. That is the ministry of presence."[5] God has uniquely placed you in the lives of your students for these important days, and you can minister to them simply by being present and available.

Boundaries

The power of relationships has been stressed often in this book. As we are building those relationships, it is absolutely crucial that they are Christ-centered and do not cross any ethical, legal, or moral lines. It seems like that should be a no-brainer, but we know those lines can get crossed and talking about it often keeps potential problems at bay. What can you do now to protect yourself, your students, and your program from things that could cause harm?

Self-Care: Working with students can be emotionally and physically taxing. Make sure that you are appropriating the time that you need to care for yourself and your family in the process. When you are "off duty," on vacation, or at special family functions, have someone appointed ahead of time to cover for you if a student needs something that is urgent.

Electronic Communication: Use programs like Remind to contact groups of students and parents. As much as possible, include parents in texts and emails to individual students. Allot certain times of day to return texts and emails, and never send things out late at night unless it is an emergency. Be clear with your students and parents about when, where, and how they should contact you outside of your normal office hours. Archive emails and texts instead of deleting them so you have a record of what was sent and received.

5. TBN, *Rick Warren Testimony: My Son Matthew's Suicide and How Ministry Flows from Deep Pain.*

Social Media: Establish a policy around what can and cannot be posted by your youth workers on social media when it comes to pictures of youth events, camps, etc. Some of this will naturally be determined by the age of the students and type of activity, but parameters need to be established upfront and revisited often. It is possible that you may have students in the foster system that are part of your group, and for their safety their pictures should never be posted.

Individual Meetings: Avoid being alone with a student, whether they are of the opposite gender or not. Have a policy that there are always two adults that stay at church until all students leave or are picked up. Ask another pastor or church volunteer to join you if a student needs to talk. If you do find yourself in a situation where a student comes to your office or classroom alone, always leave a door open and position yourself close to the doorway so someone walking by can easily look in and see you. Keep curtains and blinds open. Remember that these practices protect you just as much as they protect the student.

Physical Contact: When needed, give side hugs only and always ask if it is okay first. Fist bumps and high fives are always preferred! A student should never sit on the lap of another student, pastor, or church worker. If you have your own kids in the program, help them understand why laps are not open, even for them, during children's activities. This consistency is important.

Most importantly, keep in mind that your students will always have less boundaries than you do. It is up to you, as the adult, to establish clear expectations in these areas and stick to them. Demonstrating to your students what healthy boundaries look like and the reasons behind them are one more important lesson that you can teach your students. Boundaries do not have to be punitive or dramatic; they should be as common as brushing your teeth or putting on a seatbelt. Modeling the importance of setting boundaries can be beneficial in all areas of life.

Final Thoughts

My prayer for you, as you have been reading this book, is that you will feel empowered and well equipped to work with kids and teens in your current or future role at church or faith-based setting. Implementing even one or two of these ideas or resources each week will move your program forward in positive ways. You do not have to be perfect, just available. All of the unique gifts you possess and the challenges you have faced make you just the right person to get involved in the life of a child and point them to Jesus. Never underestimate yourself or what God can do through you.

Ultimately, it is our job to plant seeds and it is God—the master gardener—who will do the rest. Thank you for allowing God to work in and through you as you minister to the children and teens that come your way. God loves them so much more than you could ever fathom. Your efforts for the kingdom are not ever in vain. May you find new strength, creativity, and energy to continue this important work.

Chapter 9 Reflection Questions

1. When do my students need advice, and when should I just listen?
2. What specific skills of reflective listening can I work on this week?
3. How can I model healthy social media practices?
4. What personal boundaries do I need to establish to protect myself, my family, and my students?
5. What idea(s) from this book can I use right now?

Bibliography

Adams, Gail. *Students with OCD: A Handbook for School Personnel.* Campton Hills, IL: Pherson Creek, 2011.
American Psychiatric Association. *Diagnostic and Statistical Manual of Mental Disorders* (5th ed. text rev.). Arlington, VA: APA, 2022.
Anderson, Winifred, et al. *Negotiating the Special Education Maze: A Guide for Parents and Teachers.* 3rd ed. USA: Woodbine House, 1997.
Centers for Disease Control and Prevention. *Anxiety and Depression in Children*, 2023. https://www.cdc.gov/childrensmentalhealth/depression.html.
———. *Youth Risk Behavior Survey: Data Summary and Trends Report*, 2023. https://www.cdc.gov/healthyyouth/data/yrbs/pdf/YRBS_Data-Summary-Trends_Report2023_508.pdf.
Chetty, Raj, et al. "Social Capital and Economic Mobility." *Opportunity Insights.* August 2022.
Children and Adults with Attention-Deficit/Hyperactivity Disorder (CHADD). *About ADHD - Overview.* 2023. https://chadd.org/about-adhd/overview/#.
———. "More Fire Than Water: A Short History of ADHD." *ADHD Weekly* (October 4, 2018). Lanham, MD. https://chadd.org/adhd-weekly/more-fire-than-water-a-short-history-of-adhd.
County Health Rankings. *Children Eligible for Free or Reduced-Price Lunch.* University of Wisconsin's Population Health Institute, 2023. https://www.countyhealthrankings.org/explore-health-rankings/county-health-rankings-model/health-factors/social-economic-factors/income/children-eligible-for-free-or-reduced-price-lunch?year=2023.
Dias, Elizabeth. "Rick Warren Preaches First Sermon Since His Son's Suicide." *Time*, July 28, 2013. https://swampland.time.com/2013/07/28/rick-warren-preaches-first-sermon-since-his-sons-suicide/.
Erikson, Erik. *Identity and the Life Cycle.* New York: Norton, 1994.
Faraone, Stephen, et al. "The World Federation of ADHD International Consensus Statement: 208 Evidence-Based Conclusions about the Disorder." *Neuroscience & Biobehavioral Reviews.* 2021.

BIBLIOGRAPHY

Felitti, Vincent, et al. "Relationship of Childhood Abuse and Household Dysfunction to Many of the Leading Causes of Deaths in Adults: The Adverse Childhood Experiences (ACE) Study." *American Journal of Preventive Medicine* 14-4 (1998) 245-58.

Guarino, Kathleen. "Trauma-Sensitive Practices in Schools." REL Southwest, 2019. https://ies.ed.gov/ncee/edlabs/regions/southwest/events/pdf/Trauma_archive/Presentations/SWTPPDTrauResponsPracWebP3-508.pdf.

Hetzendorfer, Ruth. *The Pastoral Counseling Handbook: A Guide to Helping the Hurting.* Kansas City, MO: Beacon Hill, 2009.

Immigration and Nationality Act (INA) § 101(a)42A, 2004.

Individuals with Disabilities Education Act, 20 U.S.C. § 300, 2010.

Institution of Education Sciences. "Common Trauma Symptoms in Students and Helpful Strategies for Educators." Meeting Materials, April 8, 2020. https://ies.ed.gov/ncee/edlabs/regions/appalachia/events/materials/04-8-20-Handout3_common-trauma-symptoms-and-helpful-strategies-for-educators.pdf.

International OCD Foundation, *Anxiety in the Classroom.* Boston, MA, 2024. https://anxietyintheclassroom.org/

International Rescue Committee. *Refugee Children and Youth Backgrounders.* New York, 2006.

IRIS Center Peabody College. "Second Language Acquisition." Nashville: Vanderbilt University, 2024. https://iris.peabody.vanderbilt.edu/module/ell/cresource/q1/p02/.

Jensen, Eric. *Teaching with Poverty in Mind.* Alexandria, VA: ASCD, 2009.

Lee, Nikki Bodenstab, and Vasquez, Rich. "Mental Health Concerns for Teenagers Post-Covid." Nazarene Intermountain District Assembly, Session Handout. May 12, 2023.

Lorain, Peter. "Brain Development in Young Adolescents." National Education Association, (2017) 1-2.

Martin, Edwin. "The Legislative and Litigation History of Special Education." *The Future of Children* 6,1 (1996) 25-39.

McKinney-Vento Homeless Assistance Act. 42 US Code §§11431-11435, 2001.

Miller, Lisa. *The Spiritual Child: The New Science on Parenting for Health and Lifelong Thriving.* New York: Picador, 2016.

National Autism Center. *Findings and Conclusions: National Standards Project, Phase 2.* May Institute, 2015.

National Education Association. *English Language Learners.* 2023. https://www.nsea-nv.org/professional-excellence/student-engagement/english-language-learning.

Nelson, Michael. *Barack Obama: Life Before the Presidency.* UVA Miller Center, 2023. https://millercenter.org/president/obama/life-before-the-presidency.

Payne, Ruby. *A Framework for Understanding Poverty.* 6th ed. Aha! Process, Inc., 2018.

BIBLIOGRAPHY

———. "Understanding and Working with Students and Adults from Poverty." *Poverty Series*. Aha! Process, Inc, 2003. https://www.ahaprocess.com/wp-content/uploads/2013/09/Understanding-Poverty-Ruby-Payne-Poverty-Series-I-IV.pdf.

Rageliene, Tija. "Links of Adolescents Identity Development and Relationship with Peers: A Systematic Literature Review." *The Journal of the Canadian Academy of Child and Adolescent Psychiatry* 25.2 (2016) 97-105.

Rice, Kathleen, and Groves, Betsy. *Hope and Healing: A Caregiver's Guide to Helping Young Children Affected by Trauma*. Washington, DC: Zero to Three, 2005.

Sadin, Melissa. *Trauma-Informed Teaching and IEPs: Strategies for Building Student Resilience*. Alexandria, VA: ASCD, 2022.

Sears, William, and Thompson, Lynda. *The ADD Book: New Understandings, New Approaches to Parenting Your Child*. Boston: Little Brown, 1998.

Section 504, Rehabilitation Act, 29 U.S.C. § 701. 1973.

Souers, Kristin, and Hall, Pete. *Fostering Resilient Learners: Strategies for Creating a Trauma-Sensitive Classroom*. Alexandra, VA: ASCD, 2016.

Storti, Craig. *The Art of Crossing Cultures*, 3rd ed. Boston: Nicholas Brealey, 2021.

Suicide Awareness Voices of Education (SAVE). "Warning Signs of Suicide." 2024. https://www.save.org/learn/warning-signs-of-suicide/.

Trinity Broadcasting Network (TBN). *Rick Warren Testimony: My Son Matthew's Suicide and How Ministry Flows from Deep Pain*. December 21, 2022. https://www.facebook.com/PraiseOnTBN/videos/500674105495478/.

Tucker, Jennifer. *Breath as Prayer: Calm Your Anxiety, Focus Your Mind, and Renew Your Soul*. Nashville: Thomas Nelson, 2022.

U.S. Department of Health and Human Services. *Social Media and Youth Mental Health: The U.S. Surgeon General's Advisory*, 2023. https://www.hhs.gov/surgeongeneral/priorities/youth-mental-health/social-media/index.html.

Van Reken, Ruth, et al. *Third Culture Kids 3rd Edition: Growing Up Among Worlds*. Boston: Nicholas Brealey, 2017.

Yell, Mitchell. *The Law and Special Education*. 3rd ed. Upper Saddle River, NJ: Merrill/Prentice Hall, 2012.

www.ingramcontent.com/pod-product-compliance
Lightning Source LLC
Chambersburg PA
CBHW071215160426
43196CB00012B/2308